THE ROLE OF A UNIVERSITY CHAPLAIN

Campus Faith

Dr. Maxwell Shimba

Printed in the United States of America

TABLE OF CONTENTS

INTRODUCTION

Welcome to "Campus Faith: The Role of a University Chaplain." This book aims to explore the multifaceted and indispensable role of university chaplains in the dynamic environment of higher education. University chaplains play a crucial part in fostering spiritual growth, emotional well-being, and ethical integrity among students, faculty, and staff.

The Unique Role of Chaplains

University chaplains serve as spiritual guides, counselors, advocates, and educators. They create inclusive spaces where individuals from diverse backgrounds can find support, share their experiences, and grow both personally and spiritually. Chaplains are often called upon to navigate complex ethical dilemmas, provide crisis intervention, and advocate for social justice, making their role both challenging and rewarding.

Addressing Diverse Needs

In an increasingly diverse and rapidly changing academic landscape, the responsibilities of chaplains are expanding. They support a wide range of needs, from mental health and emotional well-being to interfaith dialogue and cultural competency. Chaplains also play a pivotal role in integrating spiritual and ethical considerations into the fabric of university life, ensuring that higher education is a holistic and transformative experience.

Adapting to Change

As universities evolve, so too must the role of chaplains. The rise of digital technology, increasing diversity, and new social challenges require chaplains to adapt and innovate. This book highlights how chaplains are leveraging digital tools, embracing inclusivity, and expanding their roles to meet the contemporary needs of the campus community.

Celebrating Contributions

Throughout this book, we will explore the various ways chaplains contribute to the academic and personal journeys of those in their care. From providing spiritual guidance and emotional support to promoting ethical behavior and fostering community, chaplains are integral to creating a nurturing and inclusive campus environment.

A Guide for the Future

This book is not only a reflection on the current state of campus ministry but also a guide for the future. By sharing insights, case studies, and practical strategies, we aim to equip current and aspiring chaplains with the knowledge and tools needed to continue making a positive impact in higher education.

Acknowledgments

I would like to extend my heartfelt thanks to all the university chaplains, students, faculty, and staff who have shared their experiences and insights for this book. Your stories and contributions have been invaluable in illustrating the profound impact of campus ministry.

As we delve into the chapters ahead, I invite you to reflect on the vital role of university chaplains and consider how we can continue to support and enhance their work in fostering a compassionate, inclusive, and ethically grounded academic community.

Dr. Maxwell Shimba
Shimba Theological Institute

DR. MAXWELL SHIMBA

CHAPTER 01

THE ESSENCE OF CAMPUS MINISTRY

The role of a university chaplain is one that blends faith, guidance, and support within the academic environment. University chaplains serve as spiritual advisors, moral compasses, and emotional supporters for students, faculty, and staff. They are entrusted with fostering an inclusive atmosphere that respects and embraces diverse beliefs and traditions.

The Essence of Campus Ministry

University chaplains are often seen as the heart of campus spirituality. Their presence is a reminder that education is not just about intellectual growth but also about nurturing the spirit. Chaplains bring a sense of peace and stability to the often hectic and stressful environment of higher education.

The essence of campus ministry lies in its ability to provide a sanctuary for individuals seeking solace, guidance, and a sense of belonging. Chaplains offer a listening ear, a comforting word, and a guiding hand to those navigating the complexities of university life.

Historical Context

The role of chaplains in educational institutions has deep historical roots. In medieval Europe, chaplains were integral to universities, offering religious instruction and moral guidance. They were often clergy members who served both the spiritual and educational needs of students and faculty.

As universities evolved, so did the role of chaplains. They became more inclusive, reflecting the growing diversity within academic communities. Today, university chaplains represent a wide range of faiths and traditions, serving not just religious needs but also providing support to those who identify as spiritual but not religious, or even secular.

Modern Responsibilities

The modern university chaplain wears many hats. They are counselors, educators, and community builders. Their responsibilities include:

1. Spiritual Guidance

Chaplains provide spiritual guidance to students, faculty, and staff. This can involve leading worship services, conducting prayer meetings, and offering spiritual direction. They help individuals explore and deepen their faith, providing a safe space for questions and doubts.

2. Counseling and Support

Chaplains offer confidential counseling and support to those dealing with personal issues, academic stress, or crises. They provide a non-judgmental space for individuals to express their concerns and receive emotional support. Whether it's a student struggling with homesickness, a faculty member dealing with loss, or a staff member facing a difficult decision, chaplains are there to provide comfort and guidance.

3. Interfaith Dialogue

In today's diverse academic environment, chaplains play a crucial role in promoting interfaith dialogue and understanding. They organize events, panel discussions, and collaborative projects that bring together individuals from different faith backgrounds. By fostering respect and understanding, chaplains help create a harmonious campus community.

4. Crisis Management

Chaplains are often called upon during times of crisis. Whether it's a natural disaster, a tragic accident, or a campus-wide emergency, chaplains provide immediate and long-term support. They help individuals and the community process grief, trauma, and loss, offering a steady presence in turbulent times.

5. Ethical Leadership

Chaplains contribute to the ethical education of the campus community. They lead discussions on moral and ethical issues, helping students develop a strong moral compass. They also advise university leadership on ethical matters, ensuring that the institution's policies and practices reflect its values.

Challenges and Rewards

The role of a university chaplain is not without its challenges. Chaplains often deal with complex and sensitive issues, requiring a great deal of empathy, patience, and wisdom. They must navigate the diverse beliefs and values of the campus community, finding ways to support everyone without compromising their own principles.

Despite these challenges, the rewards of campus ministry are profound. Chaplains have the privilege of walking alongside individuals during some of the most formative years of their lives. They witness personal growth, spiritual awakening, and the strengthening of community bonds. The impact of their work is felt not only in the present but also in the lasting memories and lessons carried forward by those they serve.

The Importance of Inclusivity

A key aspect of a chaplain's role is fostering an inclusive atmosphere on campus. Inclusivity means creating an environment where everyone feels welcome, regardless of their faith or lack thereof. Chaplains work to ensure that all voices are heard and respected, promoting a culture of mutual respect and understanding.

This commitment to inclusivity is reflected in the diverse programs and services offered by chaplains. From interfaith dialogues to secular mindfulness sessions, chaplains strive to meet the varied spiritual and emotional needs of the campus community. They also advocate for the needs of minority faith groups, ensuring they have access to appropriate spaces and resources.

Looking Ahead

As universities continue to evolve, the role of the chaplain will undoubtedly change as well. New challenges and opportunities will arise, requiring chaplains to adapt and grow. However, the core mission of campus ministry—to provide spiritual guidance, emotional support, and ethical leadership—will remain unchanged.

In the chapters that follow, we will explore the many facets of campus ministry in greater detail. We will look at the daily life of a chaplain, their involvement in campus events, and their role in promoting interfaith understanding. Through stories and case studies, we will gain a deeper appreciation for the vital work of university chaplains and the profound impact they have on the academic community.

This journey will highlight the unique blend of faith, guidance, and support that defines the role of a university chaplain. It will showcase the dedication and compassion that chaplains bring to their work, and the meaningful connections they forge with those they serve. Ultimately, it will affirm the essential role of chaplains in creating a holistic and inclusive educational experience.

The role of a university chaplain is one that blends faith, guidance, and support within the academic environment. University chaplains serve as spiritual advisors, moral compasses, and emotional supporters for students, faculty, and staff. They are entrusted with fostering an inclusive atmosphere that respects and embraces diverse beliefs and traditions.

The Multifaceted Role of a University Chaplain

University chaplains are often seen as the heart of campus spirituality. Their presence is a reminder that education is not just about intellectual growth but also about nurturing the spirit. Chaplains bring a sense of peace and stability to the often hectic and stressful environment of higher education.

The essence of campus ministry lies in its ability to provide a sanctuary for individuals seeking solace, guidance, and a sense of belonging. Chaplains offer a listening ear, a comforting word, and a guiding hand to those navigating the complexities of university life.

Daily Responsibilities

Spiritual Guidance

One of the primary responsibilities of a university chaplain is to provide spiritual guidance. This involves leading worship services, conducting prayer meetings, and offering spiritual direction. Chaplains help individuals explore and deepen their faith, providing a safe space for questions and doubts.

Case Study: A Student's Journey

Emma, a freshman at a large university, felt overwhelmed by the academic and social pressures of college life. She reached out to the university chaplain, who provided her with spiritual guidance and emotional support. Through regular meetings, the chaplain helped Emma find a sense of peace and purpose, encouraging her to explore her faith and integrate it into her daily life. Emma's journey illustrates the profound impact chaplains can have on individual students.

Counseling and Support

Chaplains offer confidential counseling and support to those dealing with personal issues, academic stress, or crises. They provide a non-judgmental space for individuals to express their concerns and receive emotional support. Whether it's a student struggling with homesickness, a faculty member dealing with loss, or a staff member facing a difficult decision, chaplains are there to provide comfort and guidance.

Story: A Faculty Member's Loss

Dr. Patel, a respected professor, lost her spouse unexpectedly. The university chaplain reached out to offer support, providing a compassionate presence during a time of immense grief. The chaplain's ongoing support helped Dr. Patel navigate her loss and continue her work, highlighting the crucial role chaplains play in supporting faculty and staff.

Interfaith Dialogue

In today's diverse academic environment, chaplains play a crucial role in promoting interfaith dialogue and understanding. They organize events, panel discussions, and collaborative projects that bring together individuals from different faith backgrounds. By fostering respect and understanding, chaplains help create a harmonious campus community.

Interview: Promoting Interfaith Understanding

Rev. John, a university chaplain with a background in interfaith work, shared his experiences in promoting interfaith dialogue. "It's about building bridges," he explained. "We create spaces where students from different faith traditions can come together, share their beliefs, and learn from one another. It enriches the campus community and fosters mutual respect."

Crisis Management

Chaplains are often called upon during times of crisis. Whether it's a natural disaster, a tragic accident, or a campus-wide emergency, chaplains provide immediate and long-term support. They help individuals and the community process grief, trauma, and loss, offering a steady presence in turbulent times.

Case Study: Responding to a Campus Tragedy

When a fire broke out in a campus residence hall, the university chaplain was among the first to respond. They provided immediate emotional support to affected students, organized memorial services, and facilitated counseling sessions. The chaplain's presence was instrumental in helping the community heal and move forward.

Ethical Leadership

Chaplains contribute to the ethical education of the campus community. They lead discussions on moral and ethical issues, helping students develop a strong moral compass. They also advise university leadership on ethical matters, ensuring that the institution's policies and practices reflect its values.

Story: Guiding Ethical Discussions

At a prestigious university, the chaplain regularly leads seminars on ethical leadership, engaging students in discussions about integrity, responsibility, and social justice. These sessions have become a cornerstone of the university's efforts to cultivate ethical leaders, demonstrating the chaplain's role in shaping the moral fabric of the institution.

Challenges and Rewards

The role of a university chaplain is not without its challenges. Chaplains often deal with complex and sensitive issues, requiring a great deal of empathy, patience, and wisdom. They must navigate the diverse beliefs and values of the campus community, finding ways to support everyone without compromising their own principles.

Despite these challenges, the rewards of campus ministry are profound. Chaplains have the privilege of walking alongside individuals during some of the most formative years of their lives. They witness personal growth, spiritual awakening, and the strengthening of community bonds. The impact of their work is felt not only in the present but also in the lasting memories and lessons carried forward by those they serve.

The Importance of Inclusivity

A key aspect of a chaplain's role is fostering an inclusive atmosphere on campus. Inclusivity means creating an environment where everyone feels welcome, regardless of their faith or lack thereof. Chaplains work to ensure that all voices are heard and respected, promoting a culture of mutual respect and understanding.

This commitment to inclusivity is reflected in the diverse programs and services offered by chaplains. From interfaith dialogues to secular mindfulness sessions, chaplains strive to meet the varied spiritual and emotional needs of the campus community. They also advocate for the needs of minority faith groups, ensuring they have access to appropriate spaces and resources.

Looking Ahead

As universities continue to evolve, the role of the chaplain will undoubtedly change as well. New challenges and opportunities will arise, requiring chaplains to adapt and grow. However, the core mission of campus ministry—to provide spiritual guidance, emotional support, and ethical leadership—will remain unchanged.

Interview: The Future of Campus Ministry

Rev. Sarah, a seasoned university chaplain, shared her vision for the future of campus ministry. "We must continue to innovate," she said. "The needs of our students are changing, and we must be flexible and responsive. But at the heart of our work is a commitment to compassion, inclusivity, and support. That will never change."

In the chapters that follow, we will explore the many facets of campus ministry in greater detail. We will look at the daily life of a chaplain, their involvement in campus events, and their role in promoting interfaith understanding. Through stories and case studies, we will gain a deeper appreciation for the vital work of university chaplains and the profound impact they have on the academic community.

This journey will highlight the unique blend of faith, guidance, and support that defines the role of a university chaplain. It will showcase the dedication and compassion that chaplains bring to their work, and the meaningful connections they forge with those they serve. Ultimately, it will affirm the essential role of chaplains in creating a holistic and inclusive educational experience.

CHAPTER 02

THE HISTORICAL ROLE OF UNIVERSITY CHAPLAINS

Historically, the presence of chaplains in universities can be traced back to medieval Europe, where they played a crucial role in the academic and spiritual lives of scholars. Initially, chaplains were primarily connected to religious institutions and served as a bridge between the church and the academic community. Over time, the role evolved to accommodate the changing landscape of higher education. Today, university chaplains not only provide spiritual care but also promote ethical behavior, foster inclusivity, and support mental health.

Early Beginnings: Medieval Europe

The Birth of Universities

The concept of the university as we know it today began to take shape in medieval Europe. Institutions such as the University of Bologna, founded in 1088, and the University of Paris, established around 1150, emerged as centers of learning. These early universities were closely linked to the church, and the presence of chaplains was integral to their function.

The Chaplain's Role

In the early days, university chaplains were primarily clergy members who provided religious instruction and pastoral care to students and faculty. They conducted daily prayers, administered sacraments, and ensured that the moral and spiritual lives of the academic community were aligned with Christian teachings. Chaplains also played a significant role in the intellectual life of the university, often engaging in theological debates and scholarly pursuits.

Case Study: The University of Paris

At the University of Paris, one of the most influential institutions of the time, chaplains were central figures. They not only led religious services but also contributed to the intellectual discourse of the university. The famous theologian Thomas Aquinas, who taught at the University of Paris, exemplified the deep connection between religious and academic life during this period.

The Renaissance and Reformation

Shifts in Thought

The Renaissance and Reformation brought significant changes to the academic and religious landscape of Europe. Humanism, with its emphasis on individual potential and critical thinking, began to influence university curricula. At the same time, the Reformation challenged the authority of the Catholic Church and introduced new religious dynamics.

Evolving Roles

During this period, the role of university chaplains began to evolve. While they continued to provide spiritual care, chaplains also started to engage more with the intellectual currents of the time. They became advocates for moral and ethical education, emphasizing the importance of personal virtue and integrity.

Story: Oxford and Cambridge

At Oxford and Cambridge, two of the oldest universities in the English-speaking world, chaplains played a pivotal role in navigating the changes brought about by the Reformation. They adapted to the new religious landscape by fostering dialogue and understanding between different Christian denominations. This period marked the beginning of a more inclusive approach to campus ministry.

The Enlightenment and Beyond

Intellectual and Spiritual Challenges

The Enlightenment, with its focus on reason and scientific inquiry, posed new challenges for university chaplains. The rise of secularism and the questioning of religious authority required chaplains to find new ways to remain relevant in the academic environment.

Adapting to Change

In response, chaplains began to broaden their scope of influence. They continued to provide spiritual care but also started to address the ethical and moral implications of scientific and intellectual advancements. Chaplains became mediators between faith and reason, helping students and faculty navigate the complexities of modern thought.

Interview: A Chaplain's Perspective

Rev. James, a university chaplain with a background in both theology and science, shared his insights on this period. "The Enlightenment was a time of great intellectual growth, but it also brought significant challenges for chaplains. We had to find ways to integrate faith with reason, showing that the two could coexist and enrich one another."

The Modern Era

Expanding Roles

In the 20th and 21st centuries, the role of university chaplains has continued to evolve. Modern chaplains are not only spiritual leaders but also advocates for mental health, ethical behavior, and inclusivity. They work to create supportive environments where all members of the academic community can thrive.

Supporting Mental Health

Mental health has become a significant focus for university chaplains in recent years. They provide counseling and support to students facing stress, anxiety, and other mental health challenges. Chaplains often collaborate with counseling services and other campus resources to ensure comprehensive care.

Promoting Inclusivity

Inclusivity is another critical aspect of modern campus ministry. Chaplains work to ensure that all students, regardless of their faith or background, feel welcome and respected. This includes advocating for the needs of minority faith groups and promoting interfaith dialogue.

Ethical Leadership

Chaplains continue to play a vital role in fostering ethical behavior within the academic community. They lead discussions on moral issues, provide guidance on ethical dilemmas, and help shape university policies to reflect values of integrity and justice.

Looking Forward

As universities continue to evolve, the role of chaplains will undoubtedly change as well. New challenges and opportunities will arise, requiring chaplains to adapt and grow. However, the core mission of campus ministry—to provide spiritual guidance, emotional support, and ethical leadership—will remain unchanged.

Future Trends

Future trends in campus ministry may include greater integration of digital technology, more emphasis on mental health and well-being, and continued efforts to promote diversity and inclusion. Chaplains will need to be innovative and flexible, finding new ways to meet the evolving needs of the academic community.

Commitment to Service

Despite the changes, the commitment to service that defines the role of the chaplain will endure. Chaplains will continue to be a source of strength, compassion, and wisdom for those they serve, helping to create a supportive and inclusive academic environment.

Historically, the presence of chaplains in universities can be traced back to medieval Europe, where they played a crucial role in the academic and spiritual lives of scholars. Initially, chaplains were primarily connected to religious institutions and served as a bridge between the church and the academic community. Over time, the role evolved to accommodate the changing landscape of higher education. Today, university chaplains not only provide spiritual care but also promote ethical behavior, foster inclusivity, and support mental health.

The Early Days

The Birth of Universities

The concept of a chaplain began in the context of Christian institutions where clerics would offer spiritual guidance to students. As universities emerged in medieval Europe, chaplains became integral in shaping the moral and ethical framework of academic life. Institutions such as the University of Bologna, founded in 1088, and the University of Paris, established around 1150, were among the first to incorporate chaplaincy into their structures. These universities were closely linked to the church, and the presence of chaplains was essential to their function.

Role and Responsibilities

In the early days, university chaplains were primarily clergy members who provided religious instruction and pastoral care to students and faculty. They conducted daily prayers, administered sacraments, and ensured that the moral and spiritual lives of the academic community were aligned with Christian teachings. Chaplains also played a significant role in the intellectual life of the university, often engaging in theological debates and scholarly pursuits.

Case Study: The University of Paris

At the University of Paris, one of the most influential institutions of the time, chaplains were central figures. They not only led religious services but also contributed to the intellectual discourse of the university. The famous theologian Thomas Aquinas, who taught at the University of Paris, exemplified the deep connection between religious and academic life during this period.

Establishing Moral and Ethical Standards

Chaplains were instrumental in establishing the moral and ethical standards of early universities. They provided guidance on issues such as academic integrity, personal conduct, and the importance of living a virtuous life. Their influence extended beyond the classroom, shaping the overall character and values of the academic community.

Story: The Influence of Chaplains

Father Bernard, a chaplain at a medieval university, was known for his emphasis on ethical behavior. He frequently delivered sermons on the importance of honesty and integrity, encouraging students to uphold these values in their academic work and personal lives. His teachings left a lasting impact on the university, fostering a culture of ethical conduct that persisted for generations.

The Role of Chaplains in Student Life

Chaplains were deeply involved in the daily lives of students. They provided spiritual guidance, emotional support, and practical advice. Students often turned to chaplains for help with personal issues, academic challenges, and questions of faith. The chaplain's office was a place of refuge and reflection, where students could find solace and direction.

Interview: A Chaplain's Perspective

Rev. James, a modern university chaplain, reflects on the historical role of chaplains. "In the early days, chaplains were the heart of the university community. They provided a sense of stability and support, helping students navigate the challenges of academic life. That role hasn't changed much over the centuries. We still aim to be a source of strength and guidance for our students."

The Renaissance and Reformation

Shifts in Thought

The Renaissance and Reformation brought significant changes to the academic and religious landscape of Europe. Humanism, with its emphasis on individual potential and critical thinking, began to influence university curricula. At the same time, the Reformation challenged the authority of the Catholic Church and introduced new religious dynamics.

Evolving Roles

During this period, the role of university chaplains began to evolve. While they continued to provide spiritual care, chaplains also started to engage more with the intellectual currents of the time. They became advocates for moral and ethical education, emphasizing the importance of personal virtue and integrity.

Story: Oxford and Cambridge

At Oxford and Cambridge, two of the oldest universities in the English-speaking world, chaplains played a pivotal role in navigating the changes brought about by the Reformation. They adapted to the new religious landscape by fostering dialogue and understanding between different Christian denominations. This period marked the beginning of a more inclusive approach to campus ministry.

The Enlightenment and Beyond

Intellectual and Spiritual Challenges

The Enlightenment, with its focus on reason and scientific inquiry, posed new challenges for university chaplains. The rise of secularism and the questioning of religious authority required chaplains to find new ways to remain relevant in the academic environment.

Adapting to Change

In response, chaplains began to broaden their scope of influence. They continued to provide spiritual care but also started to address the ethical and moral implications of scientific and intellectual advancements. Chaplains became mediators between faith and reason, helping students and faculty navigate the complexities of modern thought.

Interview: A Chaplain's Perspective

Rev. John, a university chaplain with a background in both theology and science, shared his insights on this period. "The Enlightenment was a time of great intellectual growth, but it also brought significant challenges for chaplains. We had to find ways to integrate faith with reason, showing that the two could coexist and enrich one another."

The Modern Era

Expanding Roles

In the 20th and 21st centuries, the role of university chaplains has continued to evolve. Modern chaplains are not only spiritual leaders but also advocates for mental health, ethical behavior, and inclusivity. They work to create supportive environments where all members of the academic community can thrive.

Supporting Mental Health

Mental health has become a significant focus for university chaplains in recent years. They provide counseling and support to students facing stress, anxiety, and other mental health challenges. Chaplains often collaborate with counseling services and other campus resources to ensure comprehensive care.

Case Study: Mental Health Support

When a series of student suicides rocked a large university, the chaplaincy program played a critical role in the response. Chaplains offered grief counseling, organized memorial services, and worked with mental health professionals to provide ongoing support. Their efforts helped the campus community heal and underscored the importance of chaplaincy in addressing mental health issues.

Promoting Inclusivity

Inclusivity is another critical aspect of modern campus ministry. Chaplains work to ensure that all students, regardless of their faith or background, feel welcome and respected. This includes advocating for the needs of minority faith groups and promoting interfaith dialogue.

Ethical Leadership

Chaplains continue to play a vital role in fostering ethical behavior within the academic community. They lead discussions on moral issues, provide guidance on ethical dilemmas, and help shape university policies to reflect values of integrity and justice.

Looking Forward

As universities continue to evolve, the role of chaplains will undoubtedly change as well. New challenges and opportunities will arise, requiring chaplains to adapt and grow. However, the core mission of campus ministry—to provide spiritual guidance, emotional support, and ethical leadership—will remain unchanged.

Future Trends

Future trends in campus ministry may include greater integration of digital technology, more emphasis on mental health and well-being, and continued efforts to promote diversity and inclusion. Chaplains will need to be innovative and flexible, finding new ways to meet the evolving needs of the academic community.

Commitment to Service

Despite the changes, the commitment to service that defines the role of the chaplain will endure. Chaplains will continue to be a source of strength, compassion, and wisdom for those they serve, helping to create a supportive and inclusive academic environment.

Historically, the presence of chaplains in universities can be traced back to medieval Europe, where they played a crucial role in the academic and spiritual lives of scholars. Initially, chaplains were primarily connected to religious institutions and served as a bridge between the church and the academic community. Over time, the role evolved to accommodate the changing landscape of higher education. Today, university chaplains not only provide spiritual care but also promote ethical behavior, foster inclusivity, and support mental health.

The Early Days

The Birth of Universities

The concept of a chaplain began in the context of Christian institutions where clerics would offer spiritual guidance to students. As universities emerged in medieval Europe, chaplains became integral in shaping the moral and ethical framework of academic life. Institutions such as the University of Bologna, founded in 1088, and the University of Paris, established around 1150, were among the first to incorporate chaplaincy into their structures. These universities were closely linked to the church, and the presence of chaplains was essential to their function.

Role and Responsibilities

In the early days, university chaplains were primarily clergy members who provided religious instruction and pastoral care to students and faculty. They conducted daily prayers, administered sacraments, and ensured that the moral and spiritual lives of the academic community were aligned with Christian teachings. Chaplains also played a significant role in the intellectual life of the university, often engaging in theological debates and scholarly pursuits.

Case Study: The University of Paris

At the University of Paris, one of the most influential institutions of the time, chaplains were central figures. They not only led religious services but also contributed to the intellectual discourse of the university. The famous theologian Thomas Aquinas, who taught at the University of Paris, exemplified the deep connection between religious and academic life during this period.

Establishing Moral and Ethical Standards

Chaplains were instrumental in establishing the moral and ethical standards of early universities. They provided guidance on issues such as academic integrity, personal conduct, and the importance of living a virtuous life. Their influence extended beyond the classroom, shaping the overall character and values of the academic community.

Story: The Influence of Chaplains

Father Bernard, a chaplain at a medieval university, was known for his emphasis on ethical behavior. He frequently delivered sermons on the importance of honesty and integrity, encouraging students to uphold these values in their academic work and personal lives. His teachings left a lasting impact on the university, fostering a culture of ethical conduct that persisted for generations.

The Role of Chaplains in Student Life

Chaplains were deeply involved in the daily lives of students. They provided spiritual guidance, emotional support, and practical advice. Students often turned to chaplains for help with personal issues, academic challenges, and questions of faith. The chaplain's office was a place of refuge and reflection, where students could find solace and direction.

Interview: A Chaplain's Perspective

Rev. James, a modern university chaplain, reflects on the historical role of chaplains. "In the early days, chaplains were the heart of the university community. They provided a sense of stability and support, helping students navigate the challenges of academic life. That role hasn't changed much over the centuries. We still aim to be a source of strength and guidance for our students."

The Renaissance and Reformation

Shifts in Thought

The Renaissance and Reformation brought significant changes to the academic and religious landscape of Europe. Humanism, with its emphasis on individual potential and critical thinking, began to influence university curricula. At the same time, the Reformation challenged the authority of the Catholic Church and introduced new religious dynamics.

Evolving Roles

During this period, the role of university chaplains began to evolve. While they continued to provide spiritual care, chaplains also started to engage more with the intellectual currents of the time. They became advocates for moral and ethical education, emphasizing the importance of personal virtue and integrity.

Story: Oxford and Cambridge

At Oxford and Cambridge, two of the oldest universities in the English-speaking world, chaplains played a pivotal role in navigating the changes brought about by the Reformation. They adapted to the new religious landscape by fostering dialogue and understanding between different Christian denominations. This period marked the beginning of a more inclusive approach to campus ministry.

The Enlightenment and Beyond

Intellectual and Spiritual Challenges

The Enlightenment, with its focus on reason and scientific inquiry, posed new challenges for university chaplains. The rise of secularism and the questioning of religious authority required chaplains to find new ways to remain relevant in the academic environment.

Adapting to Change

In response, chaplains began to broaden their scope of influence. They continued to provide spiritual care but also started to address the ethical and moral implications of scientific and intellectual advancements. Chaplains became mediators between faith and reason, helping students and faculty navigate the complexities of modern thought.

Interview: A Chaplain's Perspective

Rev. John, a university chaplain with a background in both theology and science, shared his insights on this period. "The Enlightenment was a time of great intellectual growth, but it also brought significant challenges for chaplains. We had to find ways to integrate faith with reason, showing that the two could coexist and enrich one another."

Modern Evolution

Expanding Beyond Christian Traditions

In modern times, the role of university chaplains has expanded beyond Christian traditions to include chaplains from various faiths and even secular spiritual advisors. This evolution reflects the growing diversity in universities and the need for inclusive spiritual support.

Case Study: A Multi-Faith Chaplaincy

At a large metropolitan university, the chaplaincy team includes representatives from several faith traditions, including Christianity, Islam, Judaism, Buddhism, and Hinduism. Additionally, there are secular spiritual advisors who provide support to students who identify as spiritual but not religious. This multi-faith approach ensures that all students have access to the spiritual care and guidance they need, regardless of their background.

Inclusivity and Diversity

Modern chaplains work diligently to create an inclusive environment where all students feel welcome. This includes advocating for the needs of minority faith groups, organizing interfaith events, and fostering dialogue between different religious communities. Chaplains also address the spiritual needs of non-religious students, offering programs that focus on mindfulness, meditation, and ethical living.

Interview: A Chaplain's Mission

Imam Rashid, a university chaplain, shared his perspective on inclusivity. "Our goal is to ensure that every student feels seen and respected. We offer a range of services and programs that cater to different spiritual needs, and we work hard to promote understanding and respect among all members of the campus community."

Mental Health and Well-Being

Mental health has become a significant focus for university chaplains. They provide counseling and support to students facing stress, anxiety, and other mental health challenges. Chaplains often collaborate with counseling services and other campus resources to ensure comprehensive care.

Story: Supporting Students' Mental Health

When Sarah, a sophomore, began experiencing severe anxiety, she turned to the university chaplain for help. The chaplain provided a safe space for Sarah to talk about her struggles, offered practical coping strategies, and connected her with additional mental health resources on campus. This holistic approach to support helped Sarah manage her anxiety and succeed academically.

Ethical Leadership and Advocacy

Chaplains continue to play a vital role in fostering ethical behavior within the academic community. They lead discussions on moral issues, provide guidance on ethical dilemmas, and help shape university policies to reflect values of integrity and justice. Chaplains also advocate for social justice and work to address systemic inequalities within the university and beyond.

Case Study: Ethical Leadership

Dr. Thompson, a university chaplain with a background in social justice advocacy, regularly leads workshops on ethical leadership and social responsibility. These workshops encourage students to think critically about their role in society and to commit to actions that promote justice and equality. Dr. Thompson's efforts have helped to cultivate a culture of ethical awareness and social engagement on campus.

Looking Forward

As universities continue to evolve, the role of chaplains will undoubtedly change as well. New challenges and opportunities will arise, requiring chaplains to adapt and grow. However, the core mission of campus ministry—to provide spiritual guidance, emotional support, and ethical leadership—will remain unchanged.

Future Trends

Future trends in campus ministry may include greater integration of digital technology, more emphasis on mental health and well-being, and continued efforts to promote diversity and inclusion. Chaplains will need to be innovative and flexible, finding new ways to meet the evolving needs of the academic community.

Commitment to Service

Despite the changes, the commitment to service that defines the role of the chaplain will endure. Chaplains will continue to be a source of strength, compassion, and wisdom for those they serve, helping to create a supportive and inclusive academic environment.

Interview: Vision for the Future

Rabbi Leah, a university chaplain, shared her vision for the future of campus ministry. "We must be proactive in addressing the changing needs of our students. This means embracing new technologies, expanding our mental health support, and continuing to foster an inclusive environment. Our role is to serve, and that means being responsive and adaptable."

CHAPTER 03

DAILY LIFE OF A UNIVERSITY CHAPLAIN

The daily life of a university chaplain is varied and dynamic. A typical day might include one-on-one counseling sessions, organizing and leading worship services, and participating in academic and administrative meetings. Each day brings new challenges and opportunities, requiring chaplains to be flexible, compassionate, and resourceful.

Morning Routine

Personal Reflection and Prayer

Many chaplains start their day with personal reflection and prayer. This time of quiet contemplation helps them center themselves and prepare for the day's responsibilities. Whether through meditation, reading sacred texts, or simply sitting in silence, this practice allows chaplains to draw strength and guidance from their faith.

Story: A Morning Ritual

Rev. Sarah begins each day with a 30-minute meditation session in her office. She lights a candle, reads a passage from her favorite spiritual book, and spends a few moments in silent prayer. This routine helps her stay grounded and focused, enabling her to approach her work with clarity and compassion.

Planning the Day

After personal reflection, chaplains often spend some time planning their day. This can include reviewing their schedule, preparing for meetings, and organizing materials for worship services or workshops. Effective time management is crucial, as chaplains juggle a wide range of responsibilities.

Case Study: A Well-Organized Day

Imam Rashid uses a detailed planner to keep track of his appointments and tasks. He starts his day by reviewing his schedule, and making sure he has all the necessary materials for his meetings and events. This organized approach allows him to handle his diverse responsibilities efficiently.

Counseling Sessions

One-on-One Counseling

One of the core responsibilities of a university chaplain is providing one-on-one counseling to students, faculty, and staff. These sessions offer a confidential space for individuals to discuss personal issues, seek spiritual guidance, and find emotional support. Chaplains listen with empathy, offer practical advice, and help individuals explore their faith and values.

Story: Supporting a Student in Crisis

When Michael, a junior, felt overwhelmed by academic pressures and personal problems, he reached out to the university chaplain. The chaplain provided a safe and supportive environment for Michael to talk about his struggles. Through regular counseling sessions, Michael learned coping strategies and gained a renewed sense of hope and direction.

Group Counseling and Workshops

In addition to one-on-one counseling, chaplains often lead group counseling sessions and workshops on various topics, such as stress management, grief support, and ethical decision-making. These group settings foster a sense of community and mutual support, helping participants feel less isolated in their struggles.

Case Study: A Stress Management Workshop

Dr. Patel, a university chaplain, organized a workshop on stress management during finals week. The workshop included mindfulness exercises, stress-reduction techniques, and group discussions. Students who attended reported feeling more relaxed and better equipped to handle their exams, highlighting the positive impact of such initiatives.

Community Engagement

Building Relationships

Building relationships with students, faculty, and staff is a key part of a chaplain's role. Chaplains often attend campus events, participate in student organization meetings, and engage in informal conversations around campus. These interactions help chaplains stay connected to the community and understand the needs and concerns of its members.

Story: Engaging with the Campus Community

Rabbi Leah makes it a point to attend as many campus events as possible, from sports games to art exhibitions. Her presence at these events allows her to connect with students and faculty in a relaxed setting, building trust and rapport. This engagement helps her better serve the community and address its diverse needs.

Organizing Events

Chaplains also organize events that promote spiritual growth, ethical reflection, and community building. These can include worship services, interfaith dialogues, social justice initiatives, and cultural celebrations. By creating opportunities for meaningful engagement, chaplains help foster a vibrant and inclusive campus community.

Case Study: An Interfaith Dialogue

Rev. John organized an interfaith dialogue event that brought together students from different religious backgrounds to discuss their beliefs and experiences. The event included panel discussions, small group conversations, and a shared meal. Participants left with a deeper understanding of each other's faiths and a renewed commitment to mutual respect and cooperation.

Administrative Duties

Participating in Meetings

University chaplains are often involved in various administrative and academic meetings. They may serve on committees related to student affairs, diversity and inclusion, mental health, and ethics. Their input helps ensure that the university's policies and practices align with its values and mission.

Interview: A Chaplain's Administrative Role

Dr. Thompson, a university chaplain, shared his experiences serving on the university's diversity and inclusion committee. "It's important for chaplains to have a voice in these discussions," he said. "We bring a unique perspective that emphasizes compassion, ethical behavior, and respect for all individuals. Our contributions can help shape a more inclusive and supportive campus environment."

Managing Resources

Chaplains also manage various resources, such as budgets, event planning, and the upkeep of worship and meditation spaces. This administrative work is essential for the smooth operation of their programs and services.

Case Study: Efficient Resource Management

Imam Rashid oversees the university's meditation center, ensuring it is well-maintained and welcoming. He manages the budget for the center, plans events, and coordinates with other campus organizations to promote its use. His efforts have made the meditation center a popular and valued resource for the campus community.

Worship Services and Spiritual Programs

Leading Worship Services

Leading worship services is a central part of a chaplain's role. These services provide a space for communal prayer, reflection, and spiritual nourishment. Chaplains often tailor services to the needs and traditions of their community, creating inclusive and meaningful experiences.

Story: A Unique Worship Service

Rev. Sarah leads a weekly worship service that incorporates elements from different Christian traditions, including contemporary music, traditional hymns, and reflective prayer. This inclusive approach attracts a diverse group of students and faculty, fostering a sense of unity and shared faith.

Spiritual Programs

Chaplains also organize various spiritual programs, such as Bible studies, meditation sessions, and retreats. These programs offer opportunities for individuals to deepen their faith, explore new spiritual practices, and connect with others who share similar interests.

Case Study: A Successful Retreat

Rabbi Leah organized a weekend retreat focused on mindfulness and spiritual renewal. The retreat included guided meditations, nature walks, and group discussions. Participants reported feeling rejuvenated and inspired, highlighting the value of such programs in supporting spiritual growth.

Crisis Management

Immediate Response

In times of crisis, university chaplains are often among the first responders. Whether it's a natural disaster, a tragic accident, or a personal crisis, chaplains provide immediate emotional and spiritual support. Their presence can be a source of comfort and stability in the midst of chaos.

Story: Responding to a Campus Crisis

When a fire broke out in a campus residence hall, Rev. John was on the scene within minutes. He provided support to displaced students, helped coordinate temporary housing, and offered prayers and comfort. His swift response and compassionate care were crucial in helping the community cope with the crisis.

Long-term Support

Chaplains also offer long-term support to individuals and the community following a crisis. This can include ongoing counseling, organizing memorial services, and facilitating support groups. Their continued presence helps individuals process their experiences and begin to heal.

Case Study: Supporting Grieving Students

After the sudden death of a beloved professor, Dr. Thompson organized a series of support groups for grieving students. These groups provided a space for students to share their feelings, support each other, and find solace in their shared grief. The chaplain's efforts helped the community navigate this difficult time and honor the professor's legacy.

Conclusion

The daily life of a university chaplain is rich and multifaceted, encompassing a wide range of responsibilities and experiences. From providing spiritual guidance and emotional support to organizing events and managing resources, chaplains play a vital role in the life of the university. Their work fosters a sense of community, promotes ethical behavior, and supports the well-being of students, faculty, and staff. As universities continue to evolve, the role of the chaplain will remain essential, adapting to meet new challenges and opportunities while staying true to its core mission of service and support.

Daily Life of a University Chaplain

The daily life of a university chaplain is varied and dynamic. A typical day might include one-on-one counseling sessions, organizing and leading worship services, and participating in academic and administrative meetings. Each day brings new challenges and opportunities, requiring chaplains to be flexible, compassionate, and resourceful.

Morning Routine

Personal Reflection and Prayer

A university chaplain often starts the day with personal reflection and prayer. This practice sets a tone of mindfulness and readiness to serve the campus community. The quiet moments of the early morning are an opportunity to center oneself, seek spiritual guidance, and prepare mentally and emotionally for the day ahead.

Story: A Morning Ritual

Rev. Sarah begins each day with a 30-minute meditation session in her office. She lights a candle, reads a passage from her favorite spiritual book, and spends a few moments in silent prayer. This routine helps her stay grounded and focused, enabling her to approach her work with clarity and compassion.

Planning the Day

After personal reflection, chaplains often spend some time planning their day. This can include reviewing their schedule, preparing for meetings, and organizing materials for worship services or workshops. Effective time management is crucial, as chaplains juggle a wide range of responsibilities.

Case Study: A Well-Organized Day

Imam Rashid uses a detailed planner to keep track of his appointments and tasks. He starts his day by reviewing his schedule, and making sure he has all the necessary materials for his meetings and events. This organized approach allows him to handle his diverse responsibilities efficiently.

Counseling Sessions

One-on-One Counseling

One of the core responsibilities of a university chaplain is providing one-on-one counseling to students, faculty, and staff. These sessions offer a confidential space for individuals to discuss personal issues, seek spiritual guidance, and find emotional support. Chaplains listen with empathy, offer practical advice, and help individuals explore their faith and values.

Story: Supporting a Student in Crisis

When Michael, a junior, felt overwhelmed by academic pressures and personal problems, he reached out to the university chaplain. The chaplain provided a safe and supportive environment for Michael to talk about his struggles. Through regular counseling sessions, Michael learned coping strategies and gained a renewed sense of hope and direction.

Group Counseling and Workshops

In addition to one-on-one counseling, chaplains often lead group counseling sessions and workshops on various topics, such as stress management, grief support, and ethical decision-making. These group settings foster a sense of community and mutual support, helping participants feel less isolated in their struggles.

Case Study: A Stress Management Workshop

Dr. Patel, a university chaplain, organized a workshop on stress management during finals week. The workshop included mindfulness exercises, stress-reduction techniques, and group discussions. Students who attended reported feeling more relaxed and better equipped to handle their exams, highlighting the positive impact of such initiatives.

Community Engagement

Building Relationships

Building relationships with students, faculty, and staff is a key part of a chaplain's role. Chaplains often attend campus events, participate in student organization meetings, and engage in informal conversations around campus. These interactions help chaplains stay connected to the community and understand the needs and concerns of its members.

Story: Engaging with the Campus Community

Rabbi Leah makes it a point to attend as many campus events as possible, from sports games to art exhibitions. Her presence at these events allows her to connect with students and faculty in a relaxed setting, building trust and rapport. This engagement helps her better serve the community and address its diverse needs.

Organizing Events

Chaplains also organize events that promote spiritual growth, ethical reflection, and community building. These can include worship services, interfaith dialogues, social justice initiatives, and cultural celebrations. By creating opportunities for meaningful engagement, chaplains help foster a vibrant and inclusive campus community.

Case Study: An Interfaith Dialogue

Rev. John organized an interfaith dialogue event that brought together students from different religious backgrounds to discuss their beliefs and experiences. The event included panel discussions, small group conversations, and a shared meal. Participants left with a deeper understanding of each other's faiths and a renewed commitment to mutual respect and cooperation.

Administrative Duties

Participating in Meetings

University chaplains are often involved in various administrative and academic meetings. They may serve on committees related to student affairs, diversity and inclusion, mental health, and ethics. Their input helps ensure that the university's policies and practices align with its values and mission.

Interview: A Chaplain's Administrative Role

Dr. Thompson, a university chaplain, shared his experiences serving on the university's diversity and inclusion committee. "It's important for chaplains to have a voice in these discussions," he said. "We bring a unique perspective that emphasizes compassion, ethical behavior, and respect for all individuals. Our contributions can help shape a more inclusive and supportive campus environment."

Managing Resources

Chaplains also manage various resources, such as budgets, event planning, and the upkeep of worship and meditation spaces. This administrative work is essential for the smooth operation of their programs and services.

Case Study: Efficient Resource Management

Imam Rashid oversees the university's meditation center, ensuring it is well-maintained and welcoming. He manages the budget for the center, plans events, and coordinates with other campus organizations to promote its use. His efforts have made the meditation center a popular and valued resource for the campus community.

Worship Services and Spiritual Programs

Leading Worship Services

Leading worship services is a central part of a chaplain's role. These services provide a space for communal prayer, reflection, and spiritual nourishment. Chaplains often tailor services to the needs and traditions of their community, creating inclusive and meaningful experiences.

Story: A Unique Worship Service

Rev. Sarah leads a weekly worship service that incorporates elements from different Christian traditions, including contemporary music, traditional hymns, and reflective prayer. This inclusive approach attracts a diverse group of students and faculty, fostering a sense of unity and shared faith.

Spiritual Programs

Chaplains also organize various spiritual programs, such as Bible studies, meditation sessions, and retreats. These programs offer opportunities for individuals to deepen their faith, explore new spiritual practices, and connect with others who share similar interests.

Case Study: A Successful Retreat

Rabbi Leah organized a weekend retreat focused on mindfulness and spiritual renewal. The retreat included guided meditations, nature walks, and group discussions. Participants reported feeling rejuvenated and inspired, highlighting the value of such programs in supporting spiritual growth.

Crisis Management

Immediate Response

In times of crisis, university chaplains are often among the first responders. Whether it's a natural disaster, a tragic accident, or a personal crisis, chaplains provide immediate emotional and spiritual support. Their presence can be a source of comfort and stability in the midst of chaos.

Story: Responding to a Campus Crisis

When a fire broke out in a campus residence hall, Rev. John was on the scene within minutes. He provided support to displaced students, helped coordinate temporary housing, and offered prayers and comfort. His swift response and compassionate care were crucial in helping the community cope with the crisis.

Long-term Support

Chaplains also offer long-term support to individuals and the community following a crisis. This can include ongoing counseling, organizing memorial services, and facilitating support groups. Their continued presence helps individuals process their experiences and begin to heal.

Case Study: Supporting Grieving Students

After the sudden death of a beloved professor, Dr. Thompson organized a series of support groups for grieving students. These groups provided a space for students to share their feelings, support each other, and find solace in their shared grief. The chaplain's efforts helped the community navigate this difficult time and honor the professor's legacy.

Conclusion

The daily life of a university chaplain is rich and multifaceted, encompassing a wide range of responsibilities and experiences. From providing spiritual guidance and emotional support to organizing events and managing resources, chaplains play a vital role in the life of the university. Their work fosters a sense of community, promotes ethical behavior, and supports the well-being of students, faculty, and staff. As universities continue to evolve, the role of the chaplain will remain essential, adapting to meet new challenges and opportunities while staying true to its core mission of service and support.

The daily life of a university chaplain is varied and dynamic. A typical day might include one-on-one counseling sessions, organizing and leading worship services, and participating in academic and administrative meetings. Each day brings new challenges and opportunities, requiring chaplains to be flexible, compassionate, and resourceful.

Counseling Sessions

Chaplains provide a safe space for students to discuss personal issues, seek advice, and find comfort. These sessions can cover a wide range of topics, from academic stress to personal faith journeys. The chaplain's role as a counselor is integral to their mission of supporting the holistic well-being of the campus community.

One-on-One Counseling

One of the core responsibilities of a university chaplain is providing one-on-one counseling to students, faculty, and staff. These sessions offer a confidential and supportive environment where individuals can openly share their concerns and seek guidance. Chaplains listen with empathy, offer practical advice, and help individuals explore their faith and values.

Story: Supporting a Student in Crisis

Michael, a junior, felt overwhelmed by academic pressures and personal problems. He reached out to the university chaplain, Rev. Sarah, for help. In their first session, Michael shared his struggles with balancing coursework, maintaining relationships, and managing his anxiety. Rev. Sarah listened attentively, offering a compassionate ear and practical coping strategies. Over the next few weeks, through regular counseling sessions, Michael learned to manage his stress and gained a renewed sense of hope and direction.

Group Counseling and Workshops

In addition to one-on-one counseling, chaplains often lead group counseling sessions and workshops on various topics, such as stress management, grief support, and ethical decision-making. These group settings foster a sense of community and mutual support, helping participants feel less isolated in their struggles.

Case Study: A Stress Management Workshop

Dr. Patel, a university chaplain, organized a workshop on stress management during finals week. The workshop included mindfulness exercises, stress-reduction techniques, and group discussions. Students who attended reported feeling more relaxed and better equipped to handle their exams, highlighting the positive impact of such initiatives.

Addressing Academic Stress

Academic stress is one of the most common issues that students bring to chaplain counseling sessions. The pressure to perform well, meet deadlines, and achieve academic goals can be overwhelming. Chaplains help students develop strategies to manage their stress, prioritize their tasks, and maintain a healthy balance between their academic and personal lives.

Story: Navigating Academic Pressure

Emily, a sophomore, was struggling with the demands of her engineering program. She felt constantly stressed and was on the verge of burnout. Emily turned to the university chaplain, Imam Rashid, for guidance. Through their sessions, Imam Rashid helped Emily develop a study schedule, practice mindfulness techniques, and set realistic goals. With his support, Emily learned to manage her workload more effectively and regain her confidence.

Personal Faith Journeys

Many students seek out chaplains to discuss their personal faith journeys. Whether they are exploring their beliefs, experiencing a crisis of faith, or seeking to deepen their spiritual practice, chaplains provide a non-judgmental space for these conversations. They offer guidance, resources, and support to help students navigate their spiritual paths.

Case Study: Exploring Faith

Josh, a freshman, was raised in a religious household but began to question his beliefs upon entering university. He felt conflicted and unsure about his faith. Josh decided to meet with the university chaplain, Rabbi Leah, to explore his doubts. Through their discussions, Rabbi Leah provided Josh with various perspectives, encouraged him to read different religious texts, and invited him to attend interfaith events. Over time, Josh found clarity and developed a more personal and meaningful understanding of his faith.

Crisis Counseling

Chaplains are often called upon to provide crisis counseling in emergency situations, such as the death of a student, a natural disaster, or a personal crisis. They offer immediate emotional and spiritual support, helping individuals and the community cope with grief, trauma, and loss.

Story: Responding to a Personal Crisis

When Laura, a graduate student, experienced the sudden loss of a family member, she felt devastated and alone. She reached out to the university chaplain, Dr. Thompson, for support. Dr. Thompson provided a safe space for Laura to express her grief, offered comforting words, and connected her with additional resources, such as grief support groups and professional counseling. His compassionate care helped Laura navigate her loss and begin the healing process.

Ethical and Moral Guidance

Chaplains also provide guidance on ethical and moral issues that students may face. This can include dilemmas related to academic integrity, personal relationships, and social justice. Chaplains help students reflect on their values, consider the consequences of their actions, and make informed and ethical decisions.

Case Study: Navigating an Ethical Dilemma

A group of students approached Rev. John, the university chaplain, with concerns about a cheating incident they had witnessed. They were unsure how to handle the situation and felt conflicted about reporting their peers. Rev. John facilitated a discussion, helping the students explore the ethical implications of their choices and the importance of academic integrity. With his guidance, the students decided to report the incident in a manner that was respectful and fair.

Supporting Faculty and Staff

Chaplains also provide counseling and support to faculty and staff, helping them manage work-related stress, navigate personal issues, and explore their spiritual journeys. This support contributes to the overall well-being of the university community and fosters a positive and collaborative work environment.

Story: Faculty Support

Dr. Anderson, a professor, was experiencing burnout from her heavy teaching load and research responsibilities. She sought help from the university chaplain, Imam Rashid, who offered a listening ear and practical advice on self-care and work-life balance. Through their sessions, Dr. Anderson learned to set boundaries, prioritize her well-being, and find renewed passion for her work.

Counseling sessions are a crucial aspect of a university chaplain's daily life. By providing a safe and supportive space for individuals to discuss personal issues, seek advice, and find comfort, chaplains play a vital role in promoting the holistic well-being of the campus community. Whether addressing academic stress, personal faith journeys, crisis situations, or ethical dilemmas, chaplains offer compassionate care and guidance, helping individuals navigate their challenges and find meaning and purpose in their lives.

The daily life of a university chaplain is varied and dynamic. A typical day might include one-on-one counseling sessions, organizing and leading worship services, and participating in academic and administrative meetings. Each day brings new challenges and opportunities, requiring chaplains to be flexible, compassionate, and resourceful.

Community Engagement

Part of a chaplain's role involves engaging with the broader campus community. This can include attending events, collaborating with student organizations, and fostering interfaith dialogues. Community engagement is essential for building relationships, creating a sense of belonging, and promoting a culture of inclusivity and mutual respect on campus.

Building Relationships

Attending Campus Events

Building relationships with students, faculty, and staff is a key part of a chaplain's role. One effective way to do this is by attending a wide range of campus events. From sports games and art exhibitions to lectures and social gatherings, chaplains make it a point to be present and approachable.

Story: Engaging with the Campus Community

Rabbi Leah makes it a point to attend as many campus events as possible. Whether it's a basketball game, a theater performance, or a student club fair, her presence at these events allows her to connect with students and faculty in a relaxed setting. By being visible and engaged, she builds trust and rapport, making it easier for students to approach her when they need support.

Participating in Student Organizations

Another way chaplains engage with the community is by participating in student organization meetings and activities. This involvement helps chaplains stay connected to the interests and concerns of the student body and provides opportunities for meaningful interactions.

Case Study: Collaborating with Student Organizations

Imam Rashid regularly attends meetings of the university's Muslim Student Association (MSA) and other faith-based student groups. He offers guidance, supports their initiatives, and collaborates on events that promote spiritual growth and community building. His active participation strengthens the relationship between the chaplaincy and student organizations, fostering a supportive and inclusive campus environment.

Organizing Events

Chaplains also organize events that promote spiritual growth, ethical reflection, and community building. These can include worship services, interfaith dialogues, social justice initiatives, and cultural celebrations. By creating opportunities for meaningful engagement, chaplains help foster a vibrant and inclusive campus community.

Case Study: An Interfaith Dialogue

Rev. John organized an interfaith dialogue event that brought together students from different religious backgrounds to discuss their beliefs and experiences. The event included panel discussions, small group conversations, and a shared meal. Participants left with a deeper understanding of each other's faiths and a renewed commitment to mutual respect and cooperation.

Fostering Interfaith Dialogue

Promoting Mutual Understanding

In today's diverse academic environment, fostering interfaith dialogue is a crucial aspect of a chaplain's role. Chaplains organize and facilitate events that encourage students from different religious and spiritual backgrounds to engage in open and respectful conversations. These dialogues promote mutual understanding, reduce prejudice, and build a sense of unity within the campus community.

Interview: The Impact of Interfaith Dialogue

Rev. Sarah shared her experiences organizing interfaith dialogues. "These conversations are incredibly powerful," she said. "They provide a platform for students to share their beliefs, learn from one another, and find common ground. It's amazing to see the friendships and collaborations that emerge from these dialogues."

Creating Safe Spaces

Chaplains also work to create safe spaces where individuals feel comfortable sharing their beliefs and experiences. This can involve setting ground rules for respectful dialogue, providing resources on different faith traditions, and ensuring that all voices are heard and valued.

Case Study: An Inclusive Interfaith Event

Rabbi Leah organized an interfaith event called "Stories of Faith," where students from various religious backgrounds shared personal stories about their faith journeys. The event was held in a neutral, welcoming space, and ground rules were established to ensure respectful listening and dialogue. The positive feedback from participants highlighted the importance of creating safe spaces for interfaith engagement.

Collaborating with Campus Partners

Working with Academic Departments

Collaboration with academic departments is another way chaplains engage with the campus community. By partnering with faculty and staff, chaplains can integrate spiritual and ethical perspectives into the academic experience, enriching the educational environment.

Story: Integrating Ethics into the Curriculum

Dr. Thompson, a university chaplain, worked with the philosophy department to develop a series of lectures on ethics and morality. These lectures were incorporated into existing courses and provided students with opportunities to explore ethical issues from a spiritual perspective. The collaboration was well-received and highlighted the value of integrating chaplaincy into the academic experience.

Partnering with Student Services

Chaplains often collaborate with other student services, such as counseling centers, diversity offices, and residential life, to provide comprehensive support to the campus community. These partnerships help ensure that students receive holistic care that addresses their spiritual, emotional, and social needs.

Case Study: A Holistic Approach to Student Support

Imam Rashid partnered with the university's counseling center to develop a wellness program that included mental health workshops, spiritual retreats, and stress-relief activities. The program aimed to support students' overall well-being and foster a culture of self-care. The collaboration between the chaplaincy and counseling center provided students with a more comprehensive and integrated support system.

Promoting Social Justice

Advocacy and Awareness

Promoting social justice is a key aspect of community engagement for university chaplains. Chaplains advocate for marginalized and underrepresented groups, raise awareness about social justice issues, and organize events and initiatives that promote equity and inclusion.

Story: Advocating for Social Justice

Rev. John led a campaign to raise awareness about food insecurity among students. He organized a series of events, including panel discussions, fundraising drives, and volunteer opportunities at local food banks. The campaign not only provided much-needed support to students in need but also fostered a greater sense of community and social responsibility on campus.

Engaging in Service Projects

Chaplains also engage in and promote service projects that benefit the broader community. These projects provide students with opportunities to give back, develop empathy, and build connections with others.

Case Study: A Community Service Initiative

Rabbi Leah organized a community service project where students volunteered at a local homeless shelter. The project included preparing and serving meals, organizing donations, and spending time with shelter residents. The experience was transformative for many students, deepening their understanding of social justice issues and inspiring them to continue serving their community.

Community engagement is a vital component of a university chaplain's daily life. By attending events, collaborating with student organizations, fostering interfaith dialogues, and promoting social justice, chaplains build relationships and create a sense of belonging within the campus community. Their efforts to engage with the broader campus community not only support individual students but also contribute to a more inclusive, compassionate, and connected university environment.

The daily life of a university chaplain is varied and dynamic. A typical day might include one-on-one counseling sessions, organizing and leading worship services, and participating in academic and administrative meetings. Each day brings new challenges and opportunities, requiring chaplains to be flexible, compassionate, and resourceful.

Administrative Duties

Chaplains also handle a range of administrative responsibilities essential for the smooth operation of their programs and the integration of spiritual life into the campus culture. These duties include managing budgets, planning events, and working with university leadership.

Managing Budgets

Allocating Resources

One of the key administrative tasks for chaplains is managing budgets. This involves allocating resources for various programs, events, and initiatives. Chaplains must ensure that their financial planning aligns with the goals of the chaplaincy and meets the needs of the campus community.

Case Study: Efficient Budget Management

Imam Rashid oversees the budget for the university's meditation center. He meticulously tracks expenses, plans for upcoming events, and ensures that the center is well-equipped. His careful management has allowed the center to offer a wide range of programs without exceeding its budget.

Fundraising and Grants

Chaplains may also engage in fundraising activities and apply for grants to support their initiatives. This can include organizing fundraisers, writing grant proposals, and seeking donations from alumni and community members.

Story: Successful Fundraising

Rev. Sarah organized an annual fundraiser to support the chaplaincy's outreach programs. The event included a silent auction, a dinner, and performances by student groups. The fundraiser not only raised significant funds but also increased awareness about the chaplaincy's work and built stronger connections with the community.

Planning Events

Organizing Campus-Wide Events

Event planning is a significant part of a chaplain's administrative duties. Chaplains organize various events that promote spiritual growth, community building, and interfaith dialogue. This involves coordinating logistics, managing volunteers, and ensuring that events run smoothly.

Case Study: Planning a Major Event

Rabbi Leah organized a campus-wide interfaith festival that included panel discussions, workshops, and cultural performances. She coordinated with multiple departments, secured funding, and managed a team of volunteers. The festival was a huge success, attracting a large number of participants and fostering a spirit of inclusivity and mutual respect.

Regular Worship Services

In addition to special events, chaplains plan and lead regular worship services. This includes preparing sermons, selecting music, and coordinating with other clergy or student leaders. These services provide a consistent spiritual touchpoint for the campus community.

Story: Weekly Worship Planning

Rev. John leads a weekly worship service that draws students and faculty from diverse backgrounds. Each week, he carefully plans the service, selecting themes and readings that resonate with the community. His thoughtful preparation ensures that the services are meaningful and uplifting.

Collaborating with University Leadership

Integrating Spiritual Life

Chaplains work closely with university leadership to integrate spiritual life into the broader campus culture. This involves participating in strategic planning, serving on committees, and advising on policies that affect the spiritual well-being of the community.

Interview: A Chaplain's Strategic Role

Dr. Thompson, a university chaplain, shared his experiences working with university leadership. "Being part of the university's strategic planning process allows me to advocate for the spiritual needs of the community. It's important to ensure that our policies and programs reflect our commitment to holistic education and well-being."

Serving on Committees

Chaplains often serve on various university committees related to student affairs, diversity and inclusion, mental health, and ethics. Their input helps shape policies and programs that align with the university's values and mission.

Case Study: Committee Involvement

Imam Rashid serves on the university's diversity and inclusion committee. His insights and advocacy have been instrumental in developing initiatives that promote a more inclusive campus environment. His work on the committee has also strengthened the relationship between the chaplaincy and other university departments.

Policy Development

Chaplains contribute to the development and review of university policies, ensuring that they support the spiritual and ethical development of students. This can include policies on religious accommodations, ethical behavior, and mental health support.

Story: Influencing Policy

Rev. Sarah played a key role in developing a policy on religious accommodations for students. She worked with university administrators to ensure that the policy was inclusive and respectful of all faith traditions. Her efforts resulted in a comprehensive policy that supports the diverse religious needs of the student body.

Managing Chaplaincy Staff and Volunteers

Staff Supervision

Chaplains may supervise a team of assistant chaplains, administrative staff, and student interns. Effective management of this team is essential for the smooth operation of the chaplaincy. This includes delegating tasks, providing training, and conducting performance evaluations.

Case Study: Leading a Team

Rabbi Leah oversees a team of assistant chaplains and student interns. She holds regular team meetings to coordinate efforts, provide guidance, and address any challenges. Her leadership ensures that the team works efficiently and effectively to support the chaplaincy's mission.

Volunteer Coordination

Many chaplaincy programs rely on volunteers to support their initiatives. Chaplains are responsible for recruiting, training, and managing these volunteers. This involves creating volunteer opportunities, providing orientation and training, and recognizing their contributions.

Story: Volunteer Engagement

Rev. John coordinates a volunteer program that involves students in planning and leading community service projects. He provides training and support to ensure that volunteers feel prepared and valued. The program not only enhances the chaplaincy's outreach efforts but also fosters a sense of community and shared purpose among the volunteers.

Administrative duties are a crucial aspect of a university chaplain's daily life. Managing budgets, planning events, collaborating with university leadership, and overseeing staff and volunteers are all essential for the effective operation of the chaplaincy. These responsibilities ensure that the chaplaincy can provide comprehensive support to the campus community, fostering a holistic and inclusive environment. By handling these administrative tasks efficiently, chaplains can focus on their core mission of spiritual guidance, emotional support, and ethical leadership.

CHAPTER 04

SPIRITUAL GUIDANCE AND COUNSELING

University chaplains offer one-on-one counseling to students, faculty, and staff. These sessions provide a confidential space for individuals to explore their spiritual beliefs, seek guidance on personal issues, and receive emotional support. The chaplain's role as a counselor is central to their mission of fostering the spiritual and emotional well-being of the campus community.

One-on-One Counseling

The Confidential Space

One-on-one counseling sessions are a cornerstone of a chaplain's work. These sessions offer a safe and confidential environment where individuals can openly share their concerns and seek guidance. Chaplains are trained to listen empathetically, offer practical advice, and help individuals explore their faith and values.

Story: Supporting a Student in Crisis

Michael, a junior, felt overwhelmed by academic pressures and personal problems. He reached out to the university chaplain, Rev. Sarah, for help. In their first session, Michael shared his struggles with balancing coursework, maintaining relationships, and managing his anxiety. Rev. Sarah listened attentively, offering a compassionate ear and practical coping strategies. Over the next few weeks, through regular counseling sessions, Michael learned to manage his stress and gained a renewed sense of hope and direction.

Addressing Academic Stress

Academic stress is one of the most common issues that students bring to chaplain counseling sessions. The pressure to perform well, meet deadlines, and achieve academic goals can be overwhelming. Chaplains help students develop strategies to manage their stress, prioritize their tasks, and maintain a healthy balance between their academic and personal lives.

Story: Navigating Academic Pressure

Emily, a sophomore, was struggling with the demands of her engineering program. She felt constantly stressed and was on the verge of burnout. Emily turned to the university chaplain, Imam Rashid, for guidance. Through their sessions, Imam Rashid helped Emily develop a study schedule, practice mindfulness techniques and set realistic goals. With his support, Emily learned to manage her workload more effectively and regain her confidence.

Exploring Personal Faith Journeys

Many students seek out chaplains to discuss their personal faith journeys. Whether they are exploring their beliefs, experiencing a crisis of faith, or seeking to deepen their spiritual practice, chaplains provide a non-judgmental space for these conversations. They offer guidance, resources, and support to help students navigate their spiritual paths.

Case Study: Exploring Faith

Josh, a freshman, was raised in a religious household but began to question his beliefs upon entering university. He felt conflicted and unsure about his faith. Josh decided to meet with the university chaplain, Rabbi Leah, to explore his doubts. Through their discussions, Rabbi Leah provided Josh with various perspectives, encouraged him to read different religious texts, and invited him to attend interfaith events. Over time, Josh found clarity and developed a more personal and meaningful understanding of his faith.

Crisis Counseling

Chaplains are often called upon to provide crisis counseling in emergency situations, such as the death of a student, a natural disaster, or a personal crisis. They offer immediate emotional and spiritual support, helping individuals and the community cope with grief, trauma, and loss.

Story: Responding to a Personal Crisis

When Laura, a graduate student, experienced the sudden loss of a family member, she felt devastated and alone. She reached out to the university chaplain, Dr. Thompson, for support. Dr. Thompson provided a safe space for Laura to express her grief, offered comforting words, and connected her with additional resources, such as grief support groups and professional counseling. His compassionate care helped Laura navigate her loss and begin the healing process.

Ethical and Moral Guidance

Chaplains also provide guidance on ethical and moral issues that students may face. This can include dilemmas related to academic integrity, personal relationships, and social justice. Chaplains help students reflect on their values, consider the consequences of their actions, and make informed and ethical decisions.

Case Study: Navigating an Ethical Dilemma

A group of students approached Rev. John, the university chaplain, with concerns about a cheating incident they had witnessed. They were unsure how to handle the situation and felt conflicted about reporting their peers. Rev. John facilitated a discussion, helping the students explore the ethical implications of their choices and the importance of academic integrity. With his guidance, the students decided to report the incident in a manner that was respectful and fair.

Supporting Faculty and Staff

Chaplains also provide counseling and support to faculty and staff, helping them manage work-related stress, navigate personal issues, and explore their spiritual journeys. This support contributes to the overall well-being of the university community and fosters a positive and collaborative work environment.

Story: Faculty Support

Dr. Anderson, a professor, was experiencing burnout from her heavy teaching load and research responsibilities. She sought help from the university chaplain, Imam Rashid, who offered a listening ear and practical advice on self-care and work-life balance. Through their sessions, Dr. Anderson learned to set boundaries, prioritize her well-being, and find renewed passion for her work.

Long-Term Counseling

While some counseling sessions may address immediate concerns or crises, chaplains also provide long-term counseling for ongoing issues. This can include regular check-ins, continuous support for mental health challenges, or sustained guidance for spiritual growth.

Story: Long-Term Support for Mental Health

Sophia, a senior, had been struggling with depression for several years. She started meeting with Rabbi Leah in her sophomore year and continued these sessions throughout her university career. Rabbi Leah provided consistent emotional support, helped Sophia develop coping strategies, and connected her with mental health resources. The long-term counseling relationship was crucial for Sophia's well-being and academic success.

Counseling Methods and Techniques

Chaplains use a variety of counseling methods and techniques tailored to the needs of the individual. These can include active listening, cognitive-behavioral strategies, mindfulness practices, and spiritual direction. Chaplains are trained to adapt their approach to best support each person they counsel.

Case Study: Mindfulness and Stress Reduction

Rev. John introduced mindfulness practices to a group of students experiencing high levels of stress. He led them in guided meditations and taught techniques for staying present and managing anxiety. The students reported significant reductions in stress and greater overall well-being, demonstrating the effectiveness of incorporating mindfulness into counseling sessions.

Confidentiality and Trust

Confidentiality is a cornerstone of chaplain counseling. Individuals need to trust that their conversations with the chaplain will remain private. This trust is essential for open and honest communication, allowing individuals to fully express their thoughts and feelings.

Interview: The Importance of Confidentiality

Dr. Thompson emphasized the importance of confidentiality in counseling. "Confidentiality is crucial," he said. "It creates a safe space where individuals can be vulnerable and honest. Without it, they might hold back and not receive the full benefit of counseling."

One-on-one counseling is a vital aspect of a university chaplain's role, providing a confidential and supportive space for individuals to explore their spiritual beliefs, seek guidance on personal issues, and receive emotional support. Through these sessions, chaplains address a wide range of topics, from academic stress to personal faith journeys, crises, ethical dilemmas, and faculty support. By offering compassionate care and practical guidance, chaplains help individuals navigate their challenges and find meaning and purpose in their lives. This crucial work fosters the overall well-being of the campus community, contributing to a positive and inclusive university environment.

Spiritual Guidance and Counseling

University chaplains offer one-on-one counseling to students, faculty, and staff. These sessions provide a confidential space for individuals to explore their spiritual beliefs, seek guidance on personal issues, and receive emotional support. In addition to individual counseling, chaplains often facilitate group counseling sessions and workshops that focus on various topics, fostering a sense of community and mutual support.

Group counseling sessions and workshops are essential tools for chaplains to address common issues faced by the campus community. These group settings provide opportunities for individuals to share their experiences, learn from one another, and build supportive relationships. Topics often include stress management, grief support, and ethical decision-making.

Stress Management

Identifying Stressors

Stress management workshops are among the most frequently conducted by university chaplains. These workshops help participants identify their primary stressors, which can include academic pressures, personal relationships, and future uncertainties. Recognizing these stressors is the first step toward managing them effectively.

Case Study: A Stress Management Workshop

Dr. Patel, a university chaplain, organized a workshop on stress management during finals week. The workshop included mindfulness exercises, stress-reduction techniques, and group discussions. Students who attended reported feeling more relaxed and better equipped to handle their exams, highlighting the positive impact of such initiatives.

Techniques and Strategies

During these workshops, chaplains teach various stress management techniques and strategies. These can include mindfulness practices, time management skills, relaxation exercises, and the importance of maintaining a healthy work-life balance. By providing practical tools, chaplains empower participants to manage their stress more effectively.

Story: Implementing Mindfulness Practices

Rev. John led a mindfulness workshop where he introduced students to meditation and deep breathing exercises. He guided the group through several mindfulness sessions, teaching them how to stay present and reduce anxiety. Many students found these techniques helpful and continued to practice them independently, significantly improving their ability to manage stress.

Grief Support

Navigating Loss Together

Grief support groups are another critical area where chaplains provide assistance. These groups offer a safe space for individuals who are experiencing loss to come together, share their feelings, and support each other. The communal aspect of these sessions can be particularly healing, as participants realize they are not alone in their grief.

Case Study: Grief Support Group

After the sudden death of a beloved professor, Dr. Thompson organized a grief support group for students and faculty. The group met weekly, providing a space for participants to express their sorrow, share memories, and support one another through the grieving process. The sense of community and mutual understanding helped many attendees begin to heal.

Facilitating Healing

Chaplains facilitate the healing process by encouraging open and honest conversations about grief. They may use various techniques, such as storytelling, journaling, and art therapy, to help participants express their emotions. By acknowledging and validating their grief, chaplains help individuals navigate their loss and find a path toward healing.

Story: Healing Through Storytelling

Rabbi Leah led a grief support group where participants were encouraged to share stories about their loved ones. Each person had the opportunity to talk about their loss, the impact it had on their life, and the cherished memories they held. This storytelling process helped participants honor their loved ones and find comfort in their shared experiences.

Ethical Decision-Making

Exploring Moral Dilemmas

Workshops on ethical decision-making are essential for fostering a strong sense of integrity and responsibility within the campus community. These workshops provide a forum for discussing moral dilemmas, exploring different ethical frameworks, and reflecting on personal values. Participants learn to approach ethical decisions thoughtfully and confidently.

Case Study: Ethical Leadership Workshop

Rev. Sarah organized a workshop on ethical leadership for student leaders. The workshop included discussions on various ethical dilemmas they might face, such as academic dishonesty and conflicts of interest. By exploring these scenarios, students developed a deeper understanding of ethical principles and learned strategies for making responsible decisions.

Developing Ethical Frameworks

Chaplains help participants develop their ethical frameworks by introducing philosophical and theological perspectives on ethics. They encourage critical thinking and self-reflection, guiding participants to consider the consequences of their actions and the values that should inform their decisions.

Story: Reflecting on Personal Values

Imam Rashid led an ethical decision-making workshop where he asked participants to reflect on their core values and how these values influenced their actions. Through guided discussions and reflective exercises, students gained clarity on their ethical beliefs and felt more confident in their ability to navigate moral dilemmas.

Fostering Community and Mutual Support

Building Connections

Group counseling sessions and workshops are not just about addressing specific issues; they are also about building connections and fostering a sense of community. These group settings allow participants to form supportive relationships, share their experiences, and learn from one another. The sense of belonging that emerges from these sessions is invaluable for the overall well-being of the campus community.

Case Study: Building a Supportive Network

Rabbi Leah organized a series of workshops on various topics, including stress management, grief support, and ethical decision-making. Over time, participants formed a tight-knit community, supporting each other both inside and outside the workshops. This network of support helped students feel less isolated and more connected to the campus community.

Creating Safe Spaces

Chaplains are skilled at creating safe and inclusive spaces where individuals feel comfortable sharing their thoughts and experiences. This involves setting ground rules for respectful dialogue, ensuring confidentiality, and fostering an environment of trust and mutual respect. By creating these safe spaces, chaplains enable participants to engage openly and honestly in the healing and growth process.

Story: Establishing Trust in Group Settings

Rev. John established clear guidelines for respectful communication and confidentiality at the beginning of each workshop. By doing so, he created an environment where participants felt safe to share their vulnerabilities and support each other. The trust and respect within these groups were crucial for their success and impact.

Long-Term Benefits

The benefits of group counseling sessions and workshops extend beyond the immediate outcomes. Participants often carry the skills, insights, and relationships they develop in these settings into other areas of their lives. The sense of community and mutual support fostered in these groups can have a lasting positive impact on their overall well-being and success.

Interview: The Long-Term Impact of Workshops

Dr. Thompson reflected on the long-term impact of group counseling and workshops. "I've seen students who participated in these sessions go on to become more resilient, empathetic, and ethically-minded individuals. The sense of community and the skills they develop here stay with them long after they leave the university."

Group counseling sessions and workshops are vital components of a university chaplain's work. By addressing common issues such as stress management, grief support, and ethical decision-making, chaplains provide valuable resources and foster a sense of community and mutual support. These group settings enable participants to share their experiences, learn from one another, and build lasting connections. The skills, insights, and relationships developed in these sessions contribute to the overall well-being of the campus community and help individuals navigate their challenges with confidence and resilience.

University chaplains offer a variety of services to support the spiritual and emotional well-being of students, faculty, and staff. In addition to one-on-one counseling and group workshops, chaplains provide spiritual direction, helping individuals deepen their faith and integrate their spiritual beliefs into their daily lives. This chapter explores the various ways chaplains offer spiritual direction, including prayer sessions, Bible studies, and spiritual retreats.

Spiritual Direction

The Role of Spiritual Direction

Spiritual direction is a process that involves accompanying individuals on their spiritual journey. Chaplains provide guidance, support, and resources to help individuals explore their faith, discern their spiritual path, and integrate their beliefs into their everyday lives. This process is deeply personal and can be transformative, fostering a deeper connection with one's faith and a greater sense of purpose.

Interview: The Impact of Spiritual Direction

Rev. Sarah explains the importance of spiritual direction. "Spiritual direction is about helping individuals connect more deeply with their faith. It's a journey of discovery, where we explore together what it means to live a life of faith and how to integrate that faith into daily actions and decisions. It's incredibly rewarding to see individuals grow and find deeper meaning in their lives."

Prayer Sessions

Facilitating Personal and Group Prayer

Prayer sessions are a fundamental aspect of spiritual direction. Chaplains facilitate both personal and group prayer sessions, providing a space for individuals to connect with their faith through prayer. These sessions can vary in format, including silent prayer, guided meditation, and communal prayer.

Story: Personal Prayer Guidance

Michael, a sophomore, was struggling with anxiety and sought guidance from Imam Rashid. Imam Rashid suggested incorporating daily prayer into Michael's routine as a way to find peace and focus. He taught Michael various prayer techniques and provided resources to help him develop a personal prayer practice. Over time, Michael found that prayer helped him manage his anxiety and feel more grounded.

Organizing Prayer Services

Chaplains also organize regular prayer services for the campus community. These services provide an opportunity for collective worship and spiritual reflection. They are often tailored to the needs and traditions of the community, incorporating elements from different faith practices.

Case Study: A Weekly Prayer Service

Rev. John leads a weekly prayer service that incorporates contemporary Christian music, scripture readings, and reflective prayer. The service is designed to be inclusive, welcoming students from various backgrounds. The consistent turnout and positive feedback from participants highlight the importance of these communal prayer opportunities.

Bible Studies and Scriptural Exploration

Facilitating Bible Studies

Bible studies are another key component of spiritual direction. Chaplains facilitate Bible study groups, where participants can explore scripture, discuss its meaning, and reflect on its application to their lives. These sessions often involve reading passages, group discussions, and personal reflection.

Story: Bible Study Group

Emily, a junior, joined a Bible study group led by Rabbi Leah. The group met weekly to read and discuss different passages from the Bible. Through these discussions, Emily gained a deeper understanding of the scriptures and found ways to apply their teachings to her daily life. The group also provided a sense of community and support, enriching her spiritual journey.

Exploring Other Sacred Texts

In addition to Bible studies, chaplains may facilitate the exploration of other sacred texts, depending on the diverse faith backgrounds of the campus community. This inclusive approach allows individuals from different traditions to engage with their own scriptures and learn from each other.

Case Study: Interfaith Scriptural Study

Dr. Thompson organized an interfaith scriptural study group, where participants read and discussed passages from the Bible, the Quran, and other sacred texts. This group provided a unique opportunity for interfaith dialogue and mutual understanding, fostering respect and appreciation for different faith traditions.

Spiritual Retreats

Organizing Retreats

Spiritual retreats offer individuals the opportunity to step away from their daily routines and immerse themselves in a reflective and rejuvenating environment. Chaplains organize retreats that focus on spiritual growth, prayer, and community building. These retreats can range from a single day to a full weekend and often take place in peaceful, natural settings.

Story: A Weekend Spiritual Retreat

Rabbi Leah organized a weekend retreat focused on mindfulness and spiritual renewal. The retreat included guided meditations, nature walks, group discussions, and personal reflection time. Participants found the retreat to be a transformative experience, allowing them to reconnect with their faith and return to campus feeling refreshed and inspired.

Tailoring Retreats to Different Needs

Chaplains tailor retreats to meet the diverse needs of the campus community. This can include retreats for specific groups, such as student leaders, athletes, or those experiencing particular challenges. The goal is to provide a supportive and enriching experience that addresses the unique spiritual needs of each group.

Case Study: A Retreat for Student Leaders

Rev. Sarah organized a retreat for student leaders, focusing on ethical leadership and spiritual growth. The retreat included workshops on servant leadership, reflective journaling, and team-building activities. Student leaders left the retreat with a deeper understanding of their roles and a renewed commitment to leading with integrity and compassion.

Long-Term Spiritual Guidance

Developing Ongoing Relationships

Spiritual direction often involves developing long-term relationships between chaplains and individuals. These ongoing relationships allow for continuous support and guidance, helping individuals navigate their spiritual journeys over time. Chaplains provide a consistent presence, offering wisdom and encouragement as individuals grow and evolve in their faith.

Story: Long-Term Spiritual Guidance

Josh, a senior, began meeting with Imam Rashid during his freshman year. Over the years, Imam Rashid provided continuous spiritual guidance, helping Josh navigate various challenges and deepen his faith. This long-term relationship was instrumental in Josh's personal and spiritual growth, providing a stable source of support throughout his university experience.

Encouraging Personal Reflection

Chaplains encourage individuals to engage in regular personal reflection as part of their spiritual journey. This can involve journaling, meditation, or other reflective practices that help individuals connect with their inner selves and their faith. By fostering a habit of reflection, chaplains help individuals maintain a strong and active spiritual life.

Case Study: Personal Reflection Practices

Dr. Thompson encouraged his counselees to keep a spiritual journal, where they could record their thoughts, prayers, and reflections. This practice helped individuals gain insights into their spiritual journeys and identify areas for growth. Many found that regular journaling deepened their connection with their faith and provided clarity and direction in their lives.

Spiritual direction is a vital aspect of a university chaplain's role, helping individuals deepen their faith and integrate their spiritual beliefs into their daily lives. Through prayer sessions, Bible studies, spiritual retreats, and long-term guidance, chaplains provide invaluable support and resources for the campus community. These practices foster personal growth, community building, and a deeper connection to faith, contributing to the overall well-being and spiritual enrichment of students, faculty, and staff.

CHAPTER 05

INTERFAITH DIALOGUE AND INCLUSIVITY

University chaplains play a key role in promoting interfaith understanding and dialogue. By organizing interfaith events, panel discussions, and collaborative projects, chaplains create opportunities for individuals from different religious backgrounds to come together, share their beliefs, and foster mutual respect. This chapter explores the various ways chaplains promote interfaith understanding and inclusivity on campus.

Promoting Interfaith Understanding

Organizing Interfaith Events

Creating Inclusive Spaces

One of the primary methods chaplains use to promote interfaith understanding is by organizing interfaith events. These events provide a platform for students, faculty, and staff to share their religious traditions and learn about others. By creating inclusive spaces, chaplains foster an environment where diverse beliefs are respected and celebrated.

Case Study: Interfaith Harmony Week

Rev. Sarah organized an Interfaith Harmony Week on campus, featuring a series of events such as interfaith dialogues, cultural performances, and a shared meal. Each day focused on a different faith tradition, providing opportunities for participants to learn about and appreciate the diverse religious landscape of the campus. The event culminated in a community service project that brought together individuals from various faiths, highlighting the common values of compassion and service.

Facilitating Panel Discussions

Engaging Conversations

Panel discussions are another effective way to promote interfaith understanding. Chaplains invite representatives from different religious backgrounds to participate in panels where they discuss their beliefs, practices, and perspectives on various issues. These discussions encourage open dialogue, dispel misconceptions, and build bridges between different faith communities.

Story: Interfaith Panel on Faith and Science

Rabbi Leah organized an interfaith panel discussion on the topic of faith and science. The panel included representatives from Christianity, Islam, Judaism, and secular perspectives. Each panelist shared how their faith or worldview informed their understanding of scientific discoveries and ethical considerations. The discussion sparked engaging conversations among attendees, fostering a deeper appreciation for the diverse ways faith and science intersect.

Collaborative Projects

Building Relationships Through Collaboration

Collaborative projects that involve participants from different faith traditions are another way chaplains promote interfaith understanding. These projects can range from community service initiatives to academic collaborations. Working together on common goals helps individuals build relationships and find common ground despite their religious differences.

Case Study: Interfaith Garden Project

Imam Rashid initiated an interfaith garden project where students from various religious backgrounds worked together to create a community garden on campus. The project provided a space for participants to share their agricultural traditions, discuss environmental stewardship from their faith perspectives, and collaborate on a tangible, shared goal. The garden became a symbol of unity and cooperation, and the relationships formed during the project extended beyond the garden itself.

Educational Workshops

Deepening Knowledge and Understanding

Chaplains also organize educational workshops that focus on different religious traditions, interfaith dialogue techniques, and the importance of inclusivity. These workshops provide participants with the knowledge and skills needed to engage in respectful and meaningful interfaith interactions.

Story: Workshop on Interfaith Dialogue

Dr. Thompson conducted a workshop on effective interfaith dialogue, teaching participants how to engage in conversations that are both respectful and enlightening. The workshop included role-playing exercises, discussions on active listening, and strategies for addressing sensitive topics. Participants left with greater confidence in their ability to participate in interfaith dialogues and a deeper understanding of the importance of such interactions.

Inclusivity in Worship

Creating Inclusive Worship Services

Respecting Diverse Traditions

Chaplains ensure that worship services and spiritual programs are inclusive and respectful of diverse traditions. This might involve incorporating elements from multiple faiths into services or creating separate spaces for different religious practices. Inclusive worship services help create a welcoming environment for all members of the campus community.

Case Study: Multifaith Worship Service

Rev. John organized a multifaith worship service that included readings from the Bible, the Quran, the Torah, and other sacred texts. The service also featured music from various religious traditions and moments of silent reflection. The inclusive nature of the service allowed participants from different faiths to feel respected and included, fostering a sense of unity and shared spirituality.

Providing Space for Minority Faiths

Advocacy and Support

Chaplains advocate for the needs of minority faith groups on campus, ensuring they have access to appropriate spaces for worship and the resources they need to practice their faith. This support is crucial for creating an inclusive environment where all students feel valued and respected.

Story: Establishing a Meditation Room

Rabbi Leah noticed that Buddhist and Hindu students on campus did not have a dedicated space for meditation and prayer. She advocated for the establishment of a meditation room that could be used by students of all faiths for quiet reflection and spiritual practice. The university administration supported the initiative, and the meditation room became a valuable resource for students seeking a peaceful space for spiritual activities.

Supporting Interfaith Student Organizations

Empowering Student-Led Initiatives

Chaplains support and collaborate with interfaith student organizations, empowering students to lead their own interfaith initiatives. By providing guidance, resources, and encouragement, chaplains help these organizations thrive and contribute to a more inclusive campus culture.

Case Study: Interfaith Student Council

Imam Rashid worked closely with the Interfaith Student Council, a student-led organization dedicated to promoting interfaith dialogue and understanding. He provided mentorship, helped secure funding for events, and collaborated on initiatives such as interfaith service projects and educational workshops. The council became a vibrant part of campus life, fostering a culture of inclusivity and mutual respect.

Addressing Challenges in Interfaith Dialogue

Navigating Sensitive Topics

Encouraging Respectful Dialogue

Interfaith dialogue can sometimes involve sensitive topics that require careful navigation. Chaplains play a crucial role in facilitating these conversations, ensuring that they remain respectful and constructive. They provide guidelines for dialogue, mediate conflicts, and create a safe space for participants to express their views.

Story: Addressing Sensitive Issues

Dr. Thompson facilitated a panel discussion on the topic of religious perspectives on sexuality. Recognizing the potential for conflict, he established clear guidelines for respectful dialogue and encouraged participants to listen with empathy. The discussion was challenging but ultimately productive, allowing participants to share their perspectives and learn from one another in a respectful environment.

Overcoming Prejudices and Stereotypes

Promoting Understanding and Empathy

One of the challenges in interfaith dialogue is overcoming prejudices and stereotypes. Chaplains work to educate the campus community about different faith traditions, dispel misconceptions, and promote understanding and empathy. Through ongoing dialogue and education, they help create a more inclusive and accepting campus culture.

Case Study: Dispelling Myths

Rev. Sarah organized a series of workshops aimed at dispelling myths and stereotypes about different religious groups. Each workshop focused on a specific faith tradition and included presentations, Q&A sessions, and personal stories from members of that faith. The workshops were well-attended and received positive feedback, contributing to a more informed and respectful campus community.

Long-Term Impact of Interfaith Initiatives

Building Lasting Relationships

Creating a Culture of Respect

The long-term impact of interfaith initiatives extends beyond individual events and workshops. By consistently promoting interfaith dialogue and inclusivity, chaplains help build lasting relationships and create a campus culture of respect and understanding. These efforts contribute to a more harmonious and cohesive university environment.

Story: Lasting Friendships

Rabbi Leah reflected on the long-term impact of interfaith initiatives she had organized over the years. "I've seen students who met at interfaith events go on to form lasting friendships. These relationships continue to grow and flourish even after they leave university, contributing to a more interconnected and understanding society."

Fostering Global Citizens

Preparing Students for a Diverse World

Interfaith dialogue and inclusivity initiatives also prepare students to become global citizens who can navigate and contribute to a diverse world. The skills and perspectives gained through these experiences equip students to engage with people from different backgrounds with empathy and respect.

Case Study: Preparing for a Global Society

Dr. Thompson shared how students who participated in interfaith initiatives on campus felt more prepared to work in diverse environments after graduation. "The experiences and skills they gained through interfaith dialogue have made them more adaptable, open-minded, and effective in their careers and personal lives. They are better equipped to contribute to a diverse and interconnected world."

Promoting interfaith understanding and inclusivity is a vital aspect of a university chaplain's role. Through organizing interfaith events, facilitating panel discussions, supporting student organizations, and advocating for minority faiths, chaplains create opportunities for meaningful dialogue and mutual respect. These efforts not only enrich the spiritual lives of individuals but also contribute to a more inclusive and harmonious campus community. The long-term impact of interfaith initiatives helps build lasting relationships, dispel prejudices, and prepare students to become compassionate and empathetic global citizens.

University chaplains play a key role in promoting interfaith understanding and dialogue. By organizing interfaith events, panel discussions, and collaborative projects, chaplains create opportunities for individuals from different religious backgrounds to come together, share their beliefs, and foster mutual respect. This chapter explores the various ways chaplains promote inclusivity in worship, ensuring that services and spiritual programs are inclusive and respectful of diverse traditions.

Inclusivity in Worship

Creating Inclusive Worship Services

Respecting Diverse Traditions

One of the primary responsibilities of chaplains is to ensure that worship services and spiritual programs are inclusive and respectful of diverse traditions. This involves understanding and appreciating the various religious practices represented within the campus community and incorporating elements from multiple faiths into services. By doing so, chaplains create a welcoming environment for all members of the university.

Case Study: Multifaith Worship Service

Rev. John organized a multifaith worship service that included readings from the Bible, the Quran, the Torah, and other sacred texts. The service also featured music from various religious traditions and moments of silent reflection. The inclusive nature of the service allowed participants from different faiths to feel respected and included, fostering a sense of unity and shared spirituality.

Designing Inclusive Services

Thoughtful Planning

When designing inclusive worship services, chaplains must thoughtfully plan each aspect of the service to ensure that it honors the traditions of various faiths while maintaining a cohesive and meaningful experience. This can involve selecting inclusive readings, prayers, and music that resonate with a diverse audience.

Story: Thoughtful Service Design

Rabbi Leah carefully planned a worship service that included elements from multiple religious traditions. She selected inclusive prayers, arranged for diverse musical contributions, and ensured that the service was structured in a way that allowed for participation from individuals of different faiths. The result was a harmonious and respectful service that celebrated the richness of religious diversity.

Collaborative Worship Planning

Engaging the Community

Chaplains often collaborate with members of different faith communities to plan worship services. This collaboration ensures that the services are genuinely inclusive and respectful of each tradition's unique aspects. Engaging the community in the planning process also fosters a sense of ownership and belonging among participants.

Case Study: Collaborative Service Planning

Imam Rashid collaborated with representatives from the campus's Christian, Jewish, Hindu, and Buddhist communities to plan an interfaith worship service. Each representative contributed elements from their tradition, ensuring that the service was inclusive and respectful. The collaborative planning process also strengthened relationships among the different faith groups, fostering a deeper sense of community.

Creating Separate Worship Spaces

Providing Dedicated Spaces

In addition to inclusive services, chaplains also create and maintain separate worship spaces for different religious practices. Providing dedicated spaces for specific faith traditions ensures that all students have access to the resources and environments they need for their spiritual practices.

Story: Establishing a Prayer Room

Rev. Sarah recognized the need for a dedicated prayer room for Muslim students on campus. She advocated for the establishment of a prayer room that included prayer rugs, Qurans, and other necessary items. The prayer room became a valuable resource for Muslim students, allowing them to practice their faith comfortably and consistently.

Scheduling and Accessibility

Accommodating Diverse Schedules

Chaplains ensure that worship services and spiritual programs are scheduled at times that are accessible to all members of the campus community. This includes considering the academic calendar, exam periods, and the needs of different religious observances. By accommodating diverse schedules, chaplains make it easier for students to participate in spiritual activities.

Case Study: Flexible Worship Scheduling

Dr. Thompson organized a series of worship services at different times throughout the week to accommodate students' varying schedules. By offering services in the early morning, afternoon, and evening, he ensured that more students could attend and participate in the spiritual life of the campus.

Accessibility and Inclusivity

Ensuring Physical and Emotional Accessibility

Inclusivity in worship also means ensuring that services are physically and emotionally accessible to all participants. This can involve providing accommodations for individuals with disabilities, offering services in multiple languages, and creating a welcoming environment for individuals of all backgrounds.

Story: Inclusive Worship Environment

Rabbi Leah made sure that the worship space was accessible to individuals with physical disabilities by providing ramps, accessible seating, and large-print materials. She also ensured that services were conducted in a welcoming and inclusive manner, using language that was respectful and inclusive of all participants. This attention to accessibility helped create a more inclusive and supportive worship environment.

Celebrating Religious Holidays

Honoring Diverse Traditions

Chaplains play a crucial role in recognizing and celebrating religious holidays from various traditions. By organizing events and services that honor these holidays, chaplains demonstrate respect for diverse religious practices and provide opportunities for the campus community to learn about and appreciate different traditions.

Case Study: Multifaith Holiday Celebrations

Imam Rashid organized a series of events to celebrate major religious holidays, including Christmas, Hanukkah, Eid al-Fitr, Diwali, and Vesak. Each event included educational components, cultural performances, and communal meals. These celebrations allowed students to share their traditions with others and fostered a deeper understanding and appreciation of religious diversity on campus.

Educating the Community

Promoting Religious Literacy

Chaplains also focus on educating the campus community about different religious traditions and practices. By promoting religious literacy, chaplains help reduce misunderstandings and foster a more inclusive and respectful environment.

Story: Religious Literacy Workshops

Rev. John conducted a series of workshops on religious literacy, covering topics such as the basics of different faith traditions, the significance of religious holidays, and the importance of religious tolerance. These workshops were well-received and contributed to a more informed and inclusive campus community.

Addressing Religious Bias and Discrimination

Advocating for Equity

Part of promoting inclusivity in worship involves addressing religious bias and discrimination. Chaplains advocate for policies and practices that ensure equity and respect for all religious traditions. They also provide support to individuals who experience religious discrimination.

Case Study: Addressing Religious Discrimination

Rabbi Leah worked with the university administration to address incidents of religious discrimination on campus. She advocated for the implementation of policies that protect students from religious bias and provided support to those affected by discrimination. Her efforts helped create a more equitable and respectful campus environment.

Long-Term Impact of Inclusive Worship

Building a Culture of Respect

The long-term impact of inclusive worship services and programs extends beyond individual events. By consistently promoting inclusivity and respect for diverse traditions, chaplains help build a campus culture that values and celebrates religious diversity.

Story: Long-Term Inclusivity Efforts

Dr. Thompson reflected on the long-term impact of his efforts to promote inclusivity in worship. "Over the years, I've seen how our commitment to inclusivity has transformed the campus culture. Students feel more respected and valued, and there's a greater sense of community and mutual understanding. It's incredibly rewarding to see the positive changes that inclusive worship can bring."

Fostering Global Citizens

Preparing Students for a Diverse World

Inclusive worship services also prepare students to become global citizens who can navigate and contribute to a diverse world. The experiences and skills gained through inclusive worship help students engage with people from different backgrounds with empathy and respect.

Case Study: Preparing for a Global Society

Rev. Sarah shared how students who participated in inclusive worship services felt more prepared to work in diverse environments after graduation. "The inclusivity we've fostered in our worship services has helped students develop a greater appreciation for diversity and a deeper understanding of different cultures. These skills are invaluable as they move into their careers and personal lives."

Promoting inclusivity in worship is a vital aspect of a university chaplain's role. By creating inclusive worship services, providing dedicated spaces for different religious practices, celebrating diverse religious holidays, and addressing religious bias, chaplains foster a welcoming and respectful environment for all members of the campus community. These efforts not only enrich the spiritual lives of individuals but also contribute to a more inclusive and harmonious campus culture. The long-term impact of inclusive worship helps build lasting relationships, dispel prejudices, and prepare students to become compassionate and empathetic global citizens.

University chaplains play a key role in promoting interfaith understanding and dialogue. By organizing interfaith events, panel discussions, and collaborative projects, chaplains create opportunities for individuals from different religious backgrounds to come together, share their beliefs, and foster mutual respect. This chapter explores the various ways chaplains support minority faiths on campus, ensuring they have the necessary resources and spaces to practice their beliefs.

Supporting Minority Faiths

Advocating for Space and Resources

Ensuring Access to Worship Spaces

One of the primary responsibilities of chaplains is to advocate for appropriate spaces for minority faith groups to practice their religion. This involves working with the university administration to secure locations for prayer, meditation, and other religious activities. Providing these spaces ensures that all students, regardless of their faith, have a place to connect with their spirituality.

Case Study: Establishing a Prayer Room for Muslim Students

Rev. Sarah recognized that Muslim students on campus needed a dedicated space for daily prayers. She collaborated with university administrators to establish a prayer room equipped with prayer rugs, Qurans, and an area for ablution. This space became a vital resource for Muslim students, allowing them to practice their faith conveniently and comfortably.

Providing Religious Resources

Chaplains also ensure that minority faith groups have access to necessary religious resources. This can include sacred texts, ritual items, and educational materials. By providing these resources, chaplains help students maintain their religious practices and deepen their spiritual understanding.

Story: Securing Ritual Items for Hindu Students

Rabbi Leah worked with the university library to secure ritual items and sacred texts for Hindu students. She ensured that these resources were readily available and easily accessible. This support helped Hindu students feel recognized and respected in their religious practices.

Organizing Cultural and Religious Events

Celebrating Diverse Traditions

Chaplains play a crucial role in organizing cultural and religious events that celebrate the traditions of minority faith groups. These events provide an opportunity for students to share their culture and beliefs with the broader campus community, fostering understanding and appreciation for diversity.

Case Study: Diwali Celebration

Imam Rashid organized a campus-wide Diwali celebration, complete with traditional music, dance, and food. The event included educational components that explained the significance of Diwali in Hindu culture. The celebration was well-attended and helped raise awareness and appreciation for Hindu traditions among the broader campus community.

Promoting Interfaith Participation

Chaplains encourage interfaith participation in cultural and religious events. By inviting individuals from different faith backgrounds to participate and learn about minority traditions, chaplains foster a spirit of inclusivity and mutual respect.

Story: Interfaith Participation in Ramadan Iftar

Dr. Thompson organized an iftar (breaking of the fast) during Ramadan and invited students, faculty, and staff from various religious backgrounds to attend. The event included a brief explanation of Ramadan, the significance of fasting, and the customs associated with iftar. Participants from different faiths shared a meal together, promoting interfaith understanding and camaraderie.

Providing Pastoral Care and Support

Individual and Group Support

Chaplains offer pastoral care and support to members of minority faith groups, both individually and collectively. This support can involve counseling, spiritual direction, and facilitating group discussions. Chaplains provide a safe and supportive environment for minority faith students to express their concerns and seek guidance.

Case Study: Pastoral Care for Buddhist Students

Rev. John noticed that Buddhist students on campus often felt isolated and lacked a sense of community. He began offering regular pastoral care sessions specifically for Buddhist students, where they could discuss their spiritual journeys and challenges. These sessions provided much-needed support and helped foster a stronger sense of community among Buddhist students.

Advocacy and Representation

Addressing Discrimination and Bias

Chaplains advocate for minority faith groups by addressing instances of discrimination and bias. They work with university administration to develop policies and practices that protect the rights of all students and ensure a respectful and inclusive campus environment.

Story: Addressing Religious Discrimination

Rabbi Leah worked with the university administration to address reports of religious discrimination against Jewish students. She advocated for stricter anti-discrimination policies and organized educational workshops to raise awareness about anti-Semitism. Her efforts led to the implementation of more robust policies and a campus-wide commitment to combating religious discrimination.

Representing Minority Faiths in University Decision-Making

Chaplains represent the interests of minority faith groups in university decision-making processes. They serve on committees and advisory boards, ensuring that the needs and perspectives of minority faith students are considered in university policies and programs.

Case Study: Representation on the Diversity and Inclusion Committee

Imam Rashid served on the university's Diversity and Inclusion Committee, where he advocated for the needs of minority faith groups. His involvement ensured that the committee's initiatives were inclusive of all religious traditions and addressed the unique challenges faced by minority faith students.

Promoting Religious Literacy and Understanding

Educational Workshops and Seminars

Chaplains organize educational workshops and seminars to promote religious literacy and understanding among the campus community. These events provide information about various faith traditions, dispel myths and misconceptions, and foster a culture of respect and inclusivity.

Story: Religious Literacy Workshop

Dr. Thompson organized a series of religious literacy workshops that covered different faith traditions, including Islam, Judaism, Hinduism, and Buddhism. Each workshop featured guest speakers, educational presentations, and Q&A sessions. The workshops were well-received and helped promote a more informed and respectful campus environment.

Encouraging Dialogue and Interaction

Chaplains encourage dialogue and interaction between different faith groups. By facilitating interfaith discussions and collaborative projects, chaplains help students from diverse backgrounds learn from one another and build meaningful relationships.

Case Study: Interfaith Dialogue Series

Rev. John organized an interfaith dialogue series that brought together students from various religious backgrounds to discuss topics such as faith and identity, religious practices, and social justice. The series provided a platform for open and respectful dialogue, fostering mutual understanding and respect among participants.

Supporting Minority Faith Leaders

Providing Mentorship and Resources

Chaplains support minority faith leaders on campus by providing mentorship and resources. This support helps faith leaders effectively serve their communities and contribute to the spiritual life of the university.

Story: Mentorship for a Sikh Student Leader

Rabbi Leah provided mentorship to a Sikh student leader who wanted to establish a Sikh student association on campus. She helped the students navigate the university's organizational processes, secure funding, and plan events. The support and guidance enabled the student leader to successfully establish the association and create a vibrant community for Sikh students.

Collaborating with Minority Faith Organizations

Building Strong Partnerships

Chaplains collaborate with minority faith organizations to support their initiatives and amplify their impact. These partnerships help ensure that minority faith groups have the resources and support they need to thrive on campus.

Case Study: Collaboration with the Muslim Student Association

Imam Rashid worked closely with the Muslim Student Association (MSA) to organize events, secure funding, and advocate for the needs of Muslim students. This collaboration strengthened the MSA's presence on campus and enhanced the support available to Muslim students.

Supporting minority faiths is a vital aspect of a university chaplain's role. By advocating for appropriate worship spaces, providing religious resources, organizing cultural and religious events, offering pastoral care, and promoting religious literacy, chaplains ensure that minority faith groups are respected and supported. These efforts contribute to a more inclusive and harmonious campus environment, where all students can practice their faith and feel valued. The long-term impact of supporting minority faiths helps build lasting relationships, dispel prejudices, and prepare students to become compassionate and empathetic global citizens.

CHAPTER 06

CRISIS MANAGEMENT AND SUPPORT

University chaplains play a crucial role in crisis management and support. In times of crisis, they are often among the first responders, providing immediate emotional and spiritual support. This chapter explores the various ways chaplains respond to crises, offer ongoing support, and help the campus community navigate difficult times.

Immediate Response

Being First Responders

Providing Immediate Support

In times of crisis, university chaplains are often among the first to respond. Their presence can offer immediate comfort and reassurance to those affected. Whether it's the sudden death of a student, a natural disaster, or a campus-wide emergency, chaplains provide essential emotional and spiritual support.

Case Study: Responding to a Student's Death

When a student tragically died in a car accident, Rev. Sarah was immediately called upon to provide support. She arrived at the scene to offer comfort to her grieving friends and classmates. She coordinated with the university's counseling services to ensure that everyone had access to grief counseling and organized a memorial service to honor the student's life. Her prompt and compassionate response helped the community begin the healing process.

Offering a Steady Presence

Providing Calm and Reassurance

During a crisis, chaplains offer a steady presence that can help stabilize the situation. They provide a sense of calm and reassurance, helping individuals process their emotions and begin to cope with the immediate aftermath.

Story: Natural Disaster Response

When a severe storm caused extensive damage to the university campus, Imam Rashid was on the scene to offer support. He provided a comforting presence to students who were evacuated from their dorms and worked with the university administration to ensure that emergency shelters were set up. His calm and reassuring demeanor helped students feel safer and more secure during the chaos.

Coordinating with Other Services

Collaborating for Comprehensive Support

Chaplains often collaborate with other university services, such as counseling centers, health services, and residential life staff, to provide comprehensive support during a crisis. This coordination ensures that all aspects of students' well-being are addressed.

Case Study: Collaborative Crisis Response

Dr. Thompson collaborated with the university's counseling center and health services during an outbreak of a contagious illness on campus. He helped coordinate efforts to provide medical care, counseling, and spiritual support to affected students. By working together, the chaplaincy and other services were able to offer a holistic response to the crisis.

Ongoing Support

Providing Long-Term Counseling

Addressing Grief and Trauma

After the immediate response, chaplains continue to provide long-term counseling and support to individuals affected by the crisis. This ongoing support helps individuals process their grief and trauma over time and begin to heal.

Story: Long-Term Grief Counseling

Following the death of a beloved professor, Rabbi Leah provided long-term grief counseling to students and faculty. She facilitated support groups, offered individual counseling sessions, and organized memorial services. Her continued presence and support were instrumental in helping the community cope with the loss and move forward.

Organizing Memorial Services

Honoring and Remembering

Chaplains often organize memorial services and remembrance events to honor those who have passed away. These services provide an opportunity for the community to come together, share their grief, and celebrate the lives of those they have lost.

Case Study: Memorial Service Organization

Rev. John organized a memorial service for a student who passed away unexpectedly. The service included personal reflections from friends and family, musical tributes, and a candlelight vigil. The event provided a meaningful way for the community to mourn and honor the student's memory.

Facilitating Support Groups

Building Community Support

Support groups facilitated by chaplains offer a safe space for individuals to share their experiences and support one another. These groups can be particularly helpful for those dealing with grief, trauma, or other emotional challenges following a crisis.

Story: Support Group for Survivors

Imam Rashid facilitated a support group for students who survived a campus building fire. The group met weekly to discuss their experiences, share coping strategies, and offer mutual support. The sense of community and shared understanding helped participants process their trauma and begin to heal.

Providing Spiritual Care

Addressing Spiritual Needs

In addition to emotional and psychological support, chaplains provide spiritual care to those affected by a crisis. This can include prayer, spiritual direction, and helping individuals find meaning and hope in the midst of difficult circumstances.

Case Study: Spiritual Care After a Natural Disaster

Dr. Thompson provided spiritual care to students and staff affected by a natural disaster. He offered prayers, led reflective sessions, and helped individuals explore their spiritual beliefs as a source of comfort and strength. His spiritual care helped many find hope and resilience in the face of adversity.

Crisis Preparedness

Developing Crisis Response Plans

Proactive Planning

Chaplains work with university administration to develop crisis response plans that outline procedures and protocols for various types of emergencies. These plans ensure that the university is prepared to respond effectively to crises and provide comprehensive support to those affected.

Story: Crisis Response Plan Development

Rabbi Leah collaborated with university administrators to develop a comprehensive crisis response plan. The plan included protocols for immediate response, coordination with other services, and long-term support. The proactive planning helped the university respond more effectively to subsequent crises.

Training and Drills

Preparing for Emergencies

Chaplains participate in training sessions and drills to prepare for emergency situations. These exercises help ensure that chaplains and other university staff are ready to respond quickly and effectively when a crisis occurs.

Case Study: Emergency Response Drill

Rev. John participated in an emergency response drill organized by the university. The drill simulated a campus-wide evacuation, and Rev. John played a key role in providing support and coordinating with other services. The exercise helped identify areas for improvement and ensured that the chaplaincy was prepared for real emergencies.

Building Resilience

Fostering a Culture of Preparedness

By fostering a culture of preparedness, chaplains help build resilience within the campus community. This involves educating students, faculty, and staff about crisis response procedures and encouraging proactive measures to ensure safety and well-being.

Story: Resilience Building Workshop

Imam Rashid conducted a resilience-building workshop for students, focusing on strategies for coping with stress and adversity. The workshop included practical exercises, discussions on resilience, and tips for maintaining well-being during challenging times. The proactive approach helped students feel more prepared and empowered to handle crises.

Crisis management and support are vital aspects of a university chaplain's role. By providing immediate emotional and spiritual support, offering ongoing counseling and care, and proactively preparing for emergencies, chaplains help the campus community navigate difficult times. Their compassionate presence and comprehensive support contribute to the overall resilience and well-being of students, faculty, and staff. The long-term impact of chaplains' crisis management efforts fosters a more supportive, connected, and resilient university environment.

Crisis Management and Support

University chaplains play a crucial role in crisis management and support. In times of crisis, they are often among the first responders, providing immediate emotional and spiritual support. However, their role does not end with an immediate response. Chaplains offer long-term support to those affected by crises, helping them navigate grief, trauma, and recovery. This ongoing support is crucial for the healing process and the well-being of the campus community.

Long-term Support

Addressing Grief and Trauma

Providing Long-term Counseling

After the initial crisis response, chaplains continue to offer long-term counseling and support to individuals affected by the crisis. This ongoing support helps individuals process their grief and trauma over time, allowing them to heal at their own pace.

Story: Ongoing Grief Counseling for Faculty

Following the death of a beloved faculty member, Rabbi Leah provided long-term grief counseling to colleagues and students. She offered individual counseling sessions and facilitated group discussions, creating a supportive environment where individuals could express their grief and share memories. Her continued presence and support were instrumental in helping the community cope with the loss and move forward.

Facilitating Support Groups

Building a Sense of Community

Support groups facilitated by chaplains offer a safe space for individuals to share their experiences and support one another. These groups can be particularly helpful for those dealing with grief, trauma, or other emotional challenges following a crisis.

Case Study: Support Group for Survivors of a Fire

Imam Rashid facilitated a support group for students who survived a dormitory fire. The group met weekly to discuss their experiences, share coping strategies, and offer mutual support. The sense of community and shared understanding helped participants process their trauma and begin to heal.

Organizing Memorial Services

Honoring and Remembering

Chaplains often organize memorial services and remembrance events to honor those who have passed away. These services provide an opportunity for the community to come together, share their grief, and celebrate the lives of those they have lost.

Case Study: Memorial Service for a Student

Rev. John organized a memorial service for a student who passed away unexpectedly. The service included personal reflections from friends and family, musical tributes, and a candlelight vigil. The event provided a meaningful way for the community to mourn and honor the student's memory, helping participants find closure and begin the healing process.

Providing Spiritual Care

Addressing Spiritual Needs

In addition to emotional and psychological support, chaplains provide spiritual care to those affected by a crisis. This can include prayer, spiritual direction, and helping individuals find meaning and hope in the midst of difficult circumstances.

Story: Spiritual Care After a Tragedy

Dr. Thompson provided spiritual care to students and staff affected by a tragic accident that claimed the lives of several students. He offered prayers, led reflective sessions, and helped individuals explore their spiritual beliefs as a source of comfort and strength. His spiritual care helped many find hope and resilience in the face of adversity.

Supporting Faculty and Staff

Offering Comprehensive Support

Chaplains also provide long-term support to faculty and staff affected by crises. This support helps ensure that the entire campus community, not just students, receives the care and resources needed to heal and recover.

Case Study: Faculty Support After a Crisis

Following a traumatic event that affected the entire campus, Rabbi Leah provided ongoing support to faculty members who were struggling with their own grief and the challenges of supporting their students. She facilitated support groups, offered individual counseling, and provided resources on coping with trauma. Her comprehensive support helped faculty members navigate their own healing process while continuing to fulfill their professional responsibilities.

Promoting Resilience and Recovery

Building Coping Strategies

Chaplains help individuals build coping strategies that promote resilience and recovery. This can include teaching stress management techniques, encouraging self-care practices, and providing resources for mental health and well-being.

Story: Resilience Workshops

Rev. Sarah conducted a series of resilience workshops for students affected by a campus crisis. The workshops included practical exercises, discussions on resilience, and tips for maintaining well-being during challenging times. The proactive approach helped students feel more empowered and better equipped to handle their emotions and stress.

Encouraging Community Engagement

Fostering a Supportive Environment

Chaplains encourage community engagement as a way to foster a supportive environment for recovery. This can include organizing community service projects, promoting volunteer opportunities, and encouraging participation in campus events.

Case Study: Community Service Project for Healing

Imam Rashid organized a community service project that brought together students, faculty, and staff to rebuild a community garden damaged during a natural disaster. The project provided a sense of purpose and a way for participants to contribute positively to the campus environment. The collective effort helped strengthen community bonds and promote healing.

Providing Educational Resources

Educating on Grief and Trauma

Chaplains provide educational resources to help individuals understand and navigate grief and trauma. This can include workshops, seminars, and written materials on topics such as the stages of grief, coping strategies, and self-care practices.

Story: Educational Seminar on Grief

Dr. Thompson organized an educational seminar on grief and loss, featuring guest speakers who specialized in bereavement counseling. The seminar provided valuable information on the grieving process and practical advice for coping with loss. Participants left with a better understanding of their own grief and the tools to support themselves and others.

Long-term support is a vital aspect of a university chaplain's role in crisis management. By providing ongoing counseling, facilitating support groups, organizing memorial services, and offering spiritual care, chaplains help individuals navigate grief, trauma, and recovery. Their comprehensive support promotes resilience and well-being within the campus community, fostering a supportive environment where healing can occur. The long-term impact of chaplains' efforts ensures that individuals receive the care they need to recover and thrive after a crisis.

University chaplains play a crucial role in crisis management and support. In times of crisis, they are often among the first responders, providing immediate emotional and spiritual support. However, their role also involves long-term support and preparation for potential future crises. This chapter explores the various ways chaplains engage in training and preparedness to effectively handle crisis situations, ensuring a coordinated and comprehensive response.

Training and Preparedness

Participating in Training Programs

Ongoing Professional Development

To stay prepared for crisis situations, chaplains regularly participate in training programs and professional development opportunities. These programs help chaplains develop the skills and knowledge necessary to respond effectively to various types of emergencies.

Story: Crisis Intervention Training

Rev. John attended a crisis intervention training program that focused on techniques for providing emotional and psychological support during emergencies. The program included simulations of different crisis scenarios, allowing participants to practice their response skills in a controlled environment. Rev. John found the training invaluable for improving his ability to remain calm and provide effective support during real-life crises.

Specialized Training for Different Crises

Chaplains often seek specialized training to handle specific types of crises, such as natural disasters, active shooter situations, and mental health emergencies. This specialized training ensures that chaplains are well-prepared to address the unique challenges posed by different crisis scenarios.

Case Study: Active Shooter Response Training

Imam Rashid participated in an active shooter response training program organized by the university's public safety department. The training included drills on lockdown procedures, communication strategies, and providing support to those affected by such incidents. The experience equipped Imam Rashid with the knowledge and confidence to respond effectively in the event of an active shooter situation on campus.

Collaborating with Campus Departments

Coordinated Crisis Response

Chaplains collaborate closely with other campus departments, such as counseling services, public safety, and residential life, to ensure a coordinated response to crises. This collaboration involves regular meetings, joint training sessions, and the development of comprehensive crisis response plans.

Story: Developing a Comprehensive Crisis Response Plan

Rabbi Leah worked with the university's counseling services, public safety, and residential life departments to develop a comprehensive crisis response plan. The plan outlined roles and responsibilities, communication protocols, and procedures for different types of emergencies. By involving multiple departments, the plan ensured a well-coordinated and effective response to any crisis that might arise.

Joint Training Exercises

Building Team Cohesion

Joint training exercises with other campus departments help build team cohesion and ensure that everyone involved in crisis response is familiar with their roles and responsibilities. These exercises simulate real-life scenarios, allowing participants to practice their responses and identify areas for improvement.

Case Study: Emergency Response Drill

Dr. Thompson participated in an emergency response drill organized by the university's public safety department. The drill simulated a campus-wide evacuation due to a natural disaster. Dr. Thompson and other participants practiced their response, communication, and coordination skills. The drill helped identify gaps in the response plan and provided valuable insights for improving future crisis management efforts.

Creating Crisis Response Protocols

Establishing Clear Procedures

Chaplains work with other campus departments to create clear crisis response protocols. These protocols outline the steps to be taken in different types of emergencies, ensuring a swift and organized response. Having established procedures helps reduce confusion and ensures that everyone knows their role during a crisis.

Story: Mental Health Crisis Protocol

Rev. Sarah collaborated with the university's counseling services to develop a protocol for responding to mental health crises. The protocol included steps for identifying and assessing the severity of the crisis, providing immediate support, and connecting individuals with appropriate mental health resources. The clear procedures helped ensure that students experiencing mental health emergencies received timely and effective care.

Fostering a Culture of Preparedness

Educating the Campus Community

Chaplains play a key role in fostering a culture of preparedness on campus. This involves educating students, faculty, and staff about crisis response procedures, encouraging proactive measures for safety and well-being, and promoting resilience.

Case Study: Resilience Workshops

Imam Rashid conducted a series of resilience workshops for students, focusing on strategies for coping with stress and adversity. The workshops included practical exercises, discussions on resilience, and tips for maintaining well-being during challenging times. The proactive approach helped students feel more prepared and empowered to handle crises.

Promoting Regular Training and Drills

Encouraging Participation

Chaplains encourage the campus community to participate in regular training sessions and drills. These activities help ensure that everyone is familiar with crisis response procedures and can act quickly and effectively in an emergency.

Story: Campus-Wide Safety Drill

Rabbi Leah organized a campus-wide safety drill in collaboration with public safety and residential life. The drill included evacuation procedures, communication protocols, and emergency shelter setups. By encouraging widespread participation, the drill helped ensure that students, faculty, and staff were prepared for potential crises.

Providing Resources and Information

Disseminating Educational Materials

Chaplains provide resources and information to the campus community to help individuals prepare for and respond to crises. This can include distributing educational materials, hosting informational sessions, and maintaining an online repository of crisis response resources.

Case Study: Crisis Preparedness Handbook

Dr. Thompson developed a crisis preparedness handbook that included information on different types of emergencies, steps to take in a crisis, and resources for support. The handbook was distributed to students, faculty, and staff and made available online. The comprehensive guide helped ensure that the campus community was well-informed and ready to respond to crises.

Training and preparedness are vital aspects of a university chaplain's role in crisis management. By participating in training programs, collaborating with other campus departments, creating clear crisis response protocols, and fostering a culture of preparedness, chaplains ensure that the campus community is well-equipped to handle emergencies. Their proactive efforts contribute to a safer, more resilient campus environment, ensuring that everyone is prepared to respond effectively to crises and support each other through challenging times.

CHAPTER 07

ACADEMIC AND MORAL INTEGRITY

University chaplains play a crucial role in fostering academic and moral integrity within the campus community. By integrating moral and ethical discussions into their programs, chaplains contribute to the holistic education of students, preparing them to become ethically-minded leaders and responsible global citizens. This chapter explores the various ways chaplains promote ethical education through seminars, workshops, and ongoing support.

Ethical Education

Integrating Ethical Discussions

Fostering Moral Reflection

Chaplains incorporate ethical discussions into their programs to encourage students to reflect on their values and the impact of their actions. These discussions provide a platform for students to explore complex moral issues and develop a strong ethical foundation.

Case Study: Weekly Ethical Reflection Sessions

Rev. John facilitated weekly ethical reflection sessions where students discussed contemporary moral dilemmas and their implications. Each session began with a short presentation on a specific ethical issue, followed by group discussions. These sessions helped students develop critical thinking skills and a deeper understanding of ethical principles.

Seminars on Academic Integrity

Promoting Honest Scholarship

Academic integrity is a cornerstone of a university's mission. Chaplains organize seminars and workshops that emphasize the importance of honesty, fairness, and responsibility in academic work. These programs aim to instill a sense of integrity and accountability in students.

Story: Academic Integrity Seminar

Imam Rashid organized a seminar on academic integrity that addressed issues such as plagiarism, cheating, and the responsible use of sources. Guest speakers included professors and academic advisors who shared their perspectives on maintaining integrity in academic work. The seminar concluded with a Q&A session where students could ask questions and seek advice on navigating ethical challenges in their studies.

Ethical Leadership Workshops

Developing Responsible Leaders

Chaplains also focus on developing ethical leadership skills among students. Workshops on ethical leadership explore topics such as decision-making, accountability, and the role of ethics in leadership. These programs prepare students to lead with integrity and make ethically sound decisions.

Case Study: Ethical Leadership Workshop

Rabbi Leah conducted an ethical leadership workshop for student leaders on campus. The workshop included case studies, role-playing exercises, and discussions on ethical dilemmas faced by leaders. Participants learned about the importance of transparency, accountability, and ethical decision-making in leadership roles. The workshop equipped them with the skills and knowledge to lead with integrity.

Social Justice Initiatives

Advocating for Equity and Justice

Chaplains play a vital role in promoting social justice on campus. They organize initiatives that raise awareness about social justice issues, advocate for marginalized groups, and encourage students to take action. These initiatives help create a more equitable and inclusive campus environment.

Story: Social Justice Awareness Week

Rev. Sarah organized a Social Justice Awareness Week that included events such as panel discussions, workshops, and volunteer opportunities. Topics covered included racial justice, gender equality, and environmental sustainability. The events aimed to educate students about social justice issues and inspire them to become advocates for change. The week culminated in a community service project that brought together students from diverse backgrounds to work toward a common goal.

Ethical Dilemmas in Everyday Life

Encouraging Ethical Living

Chaplains encourage students to apply ethical principles in their everyday lives. This involves exploring ethical dilemmas that arise in personal relationships, professional settings, and everyday interactions. By addressing these issues, chaplains help students develop a consistent and practical approach to ethical living.

Case Study: Everyday Ethics Workshop

Dr. Thompson led an "Everyday Ethics" workshop that explored common ethical dilemmas students might face in their daily lives. The workshop included discussions on topics such as honesty in relationships, ethical consumption, and the importance of standing up for one's values. Participants left with a better understanding of how to navigate ethical challenges in their personal and professional lives.

Mentorship and Support

Providing Ethical Guidance

Chaplains offer mentorship and support to students seeking guidance on ethical issues. This one-on-one support helps students navigate complex moral dilemmas and make informed decisions that align with their values.

Story: Mentorship on Ethical Challenges

A student approached Imam Rashid for advice on an ethical dilemma involving a group project. The student was concerned about a teammate's dishonest behavior but was unsure how to address the issue without causing conflict. Imam Rashid provided guidance on how to approach the situation with integrity and compassion, helping the student find a resolution that upheld ethical standards.

Collaborating with Faculty and Staff

Integrating Ethics into the Curriculum

Chaplains collaborate with faculty and staff to integrate ethical discussions into the academic curriculum.

This partnership ensures that ethical education is a consistent and integral part of the university experience.

Case Study: Integrating Ethics into Coursework

Rabbi Leah worked with professors in the philosophy and business departments to develop modules on ethics that were incorporated into existing courses. These modules included lectures, case studies, and assignments focused on ethical decision-making. The collaboration ensured that students received comprehensive ethical education across different disciplines.

Promoting a Culture of Integrity

Building a Respectful Community

Chaplains play a key role in promoting a culture of integrity on campus. This involves creating an environment where ethical behavior is valued and respected, and where individuals feel supported in upholding their principles.

Story: Campus-Wide Integrity Campaign

Rev. John spearheaded a campus-wide integrity campaign that included posters, workshops, and events promoting the importance of honesty, accountability, and respect. The campaign aimed to create a culture where ethical behavior was the norm and where students felt empowered to make ethical choices. The initiative helped foster a sense of community and shared responsibility for maintaining academic and moral integrity.

Addressing Ethical Violations

Providing Support and Accountability

When ethical violations occur, chaplains provide support to those involved and help facilitate accountability. This involves addressing the issue with compassion, ensuring that individuals understand the consequences of their actions, and promoting restorative practices that encourage growth and learning.

Case Study: Restorative Justice for Academic Misconduct

Dr. Thompson was involved in a restorative justice program for students who committed academic misconduct. The program included facilitated discussions between the students, affected parties, and academic advisors to address the harm caused and develop a plan for making amends. The restorative approach helped students learn from their mistakes and commit to upholding academic integrity in the future.

Promoting academic and moral integrity is a vital aspect of a university chaplain's role. Through seminars, workshops, mentorship, and collaboration with faculty, chaplains contribute to the ethical education of students.

Their efforts help create a campus culture where integrity, respect, and ethical behavior are valued and upheld. By fostering ethical reflection and action, chaplains prepare students to become responsible and ethically-minded leaders in their personal and professional lives.

University chaplains play a crucial role in fostering academic and moral integrity within the campus community. By integrating moral and ethical discussions into their programs, chaplains contribute to the holistic education of students, preparing them to become ethically-minded leaders and responsible global citizens. This chapter explores the various ways chaplains promote ethical education and provide advice on ethical issues, ensuring that the university's policies and practices align with its values and mission.

Advising on Ethical Issues

Providing Ethical Guidance to Leadership

Serving as Ethical Advisors

University chaplains often serve as ethical advisors to university leadership, offering insights and recommendations on ethical issues that arise within the institution. Their input helps ensure that the university's policies and practices align with its core values and mission, promoting a culture of integrity and ethical behavior.

Case Study: Ethical Decision-Making in University Leadership

Rev. John was invited to join the university's ethics committee, where he provided guidance on various ethical issues, including conflicts of interest, academic integrity, and equitable treatment of students and staff. His contributions helped the university leadership make informed decisions that upheld the institution's commitment to ethical standards.

Addressing Institutional Ethical Dilemmas

Navigating Complex Issues

Chaplains help university leadership navigate complex ethical dilemmas, offering a balanced perspective that considers the well-being of the entire campus community. This involves analyzing the ethical implications of potential decisions and providing recommendations that align with the university's values.

Story: Navigating a Financial Ethical Dilemma

Imam Rashid was consulted by university administrators regarding a financial decision that involved significant budget cuts to student services. He highlighted the ethical implications of the cuts, particularly their impact on vulnerable student populations. His input led to a reconsideration of the budget allocation, resulting in a more equitable solution that balanced financial constraints with the need to support all students.

Developing Ethical Policies

Crafting Guidelines and Protocols

Chaplains collaborate with university leadership to develop and implement ethical policies and protocols. These guidelines ensure that the institution's practices reflect its commitment to integrity, fairness, and respect for all members of the campus community.

Case Study: Developing an Inclusive Hiring Policy

Rabbi Leah worked with the human resources department to develop an inclusive hiring policy that emphasized diversity, equity, and non-discrimination. The policy included guidelines for creating diverse hiring committees, implementing unbiased recruitment practices, and providing training on inclusivity. Her contributions helped ensure that the university's hiring practices aligned with its values of diversity and inclusion.

Promoting Transparency and Accountability

Ensuring Ethical Oversight

Chaplains advocate for transparency and accountability in university operations. This involves promoting open communication, ensuring that decisions are made with integrity, and holding individuals and departments accountable for their actions.

Story: Promoting Transparency in Decision-Making

Dr. Thompson advised the university's board of trustees on the importance of transparency in decision-making processes. He recommended regular public reports on key decisions, open forums for community input, and clear communication channels between leadership and the campus community. His advocacy helped create a more transparent and accountable governance structure.

Supporting Ethical Committees

Participating in Ethical Review Boards

Chaplains often serve on ethical review boards and committees, where they provide input on a wide range of issues, from research ethics to student conduct. Their participation ensures that ethical considerations are thoroughly evaluated and integrated into the decision-making process.

Case Study: Serving on a Research Ethics Board

Rev. Sarah served on the university's research ethics board, where she reviewed research proposals to ensure they met ethical standards. She provided guidance on issues such as informed consent, confidentiality, and the protection of vulnerable populations. Her contributions helped maintain the integrity of the university's research practices.

Educating Leadership on Ethical Issues

Offering Training and Workshops

Chaplains provide education and training for university leadership on ethical issues, helping them understand and navigate complex moral landscapes. This includes workshops, seminars, and one-on-one consultations on topics such as ethical decision-making, leadership integrity, and the ethical implications of policy decisions.

Story: Ethical Leadership Workshop for Administrators

Rabbi Leah organized an ethical leadership workshop for university administrators, focusing on the principles of ethical decision-making and the importance of integrity in leadership roles. The workshop included case studies, interactive discussions, and practical exercises. Participants gained valuable insights into how to lead with integrity and uphold ethical standards in their roles.

Advocating for Ethical Practices

Championing Ethical Initiatives

Chaplains advocate for ethical practices across the university, championing initiatives that promote fairness, respect, and accountability. This involves identifying areas for improvement, proposing ethical solutions, and working with leadership to implement positive changes.

Case Study: Advocating for Fair Student Disciplinary Practices

Imam Rashid identified concerns with the university's student disciplinary practices, which lacked consistency and fairness. He worked with the student affairs office to develop a new disciplinary policy that emphasized restorative justice, clear guidelines, and equitable treatment for all students. His advocacy led to a more just and transparent disciplinary system.

Fostering a Culture of Integrity

Leading by Example

Chaplains lead by example, demonstrating ethical behavior in their interactions and decisions. Their commitment to integrity inspires others to uphold the same standards, fostering a campus culture where ethical behavior is valued and practiced.

Story: Leading with Integrity

Dr. Thompson's commitment to ethical behavior was evident in his daily interactions with students, faculty, and staff. Whether mediating conflicts, providing guidance, or making decisions, he consistently demonstrated fairness, respect, and integrity. His leadership set a positive example for the entire campus community, reinforcing the importance of ethical behavior.

Encouraging Ethical Dialogue

Facilitating Open Conversations

Chaplains encourage open dialogue about ethical issues, creating spaces for students, faculty, and staff to discuss and reflect on moral dilemmas. These conversations promote a deeper understanding of ethical principles and encourage the campus community to engage in ethical decision-making.

Case Study: Ethical Dialogue Series

Rev. John facilitated an ethical dialogue series where members of the campus community could discuss current ethical issues and explore different perspectives. The series included topics such as social justice, environmental responsibility, and academic integrity. The open and respectful conversations helped participants develop a more nuanced understanding of ethical issues and the importance of integrity in their actions.

Advising on ethical issues is a vital aspect of a university chaplain's role. By providing ethical guidance to university leadership, addressing institutional ethical dilemmas, developing ethical policies, and promoting transparency and accountability, chaplains help ensure that the university's practices align with its values and mission. Their contributions foster a campus culture of integrity, respect, and ethical behavior, preparing students to become responsible and ethically-minded leaders in their personal and professional lives.

University chaplains play a crucial role in fostering academic and moral integrity within the campus community. By integrating moral and ethical discussions into their programs, chaplains contribute to the holistic education of students, preparing them to become ethically-minded leaders and responsible global citizens. This chapter explores how chaplains serve as role models of ethical behavior and integrity, demonstrating the importance of living out one's values in both personal and professional life.

Role Modeling

Demonstrating Ethical Behavior

Leading by Example

Chaplains serve as role models of ethical behavior and integrity, setting an example for students, faculty, and staff. Through their actions and interactions, they demonstrate how to live out one's values consistently and authentically.

Story: Leading by Example

Rev. John is known for his unwavering commitment to integrity. Whether he is mediating a conflict, providing guidance, or making decisions, he consistently demonstrates fairness, honesty, and respect. His actions inspire those around him to uphold the same ethical standards, creating a ripple effect of positive behavior throughout the campus community.

Building Trust and Respect

Earning Confidence

By consistently demonstrating ethical behavior, chaplains build trust and respect within the campus community. Their integrity and commitment to ethical principles earn them the confidence of students, faculty, and staff, who look to them for guidance and support.

Case Study: Building Trust Through Consistency

Rabbi Leah's consistent ethical behavior has earned her the trust of the entire campus community. Students feel comfortable approaching her with their concerns, knowing that she will handle their issues with fairness and respect. Faculty and staff also value her input, seeking her advice on ethical dilemmas and policy decisions. Her reputation for integrity has made her a trusted and respected figure on campus.

Living Out Core Values

Integrating Values into Daily Life

Chaplains integrate their core values into their daily lives, demonstrating how to live authentically and ethically in both personal and professional settings. Their actions reflect their beliefs, providing a tangible example of how to embody one's values.

Story: Living Out Core Values

Imam Rashid's commitment to social justice is evident in everything he does. From advocating for marginalized groups to participating in community service projects, he lives out his values every day. His dedication to justice and equity serves as a powerful example for students, encouraging them to take action and make a difference in their own lives.

Providing Guidance and Support

Offering Ethical Advice

Chaplains provide guidance and support to individuals facing ethical dilemmas, helping them navigate complex moral issues and make decisions that align with their values. By offering practical advice and empathetic support, chaplains help individuals uphold their integrity in challenging situations.

Case Study: Offering Ethical Guidance

Dr. Thompson was approached by a student who was struggling with an ethical dilemma involving academic dishonesty. The student had discovered that a classmate had cheated on an exam but was unsure whether to report it. Dr. Thompson provided a safe space for the student to discuss their concerns and offered guidance on how to approach the situation with integrity and compassion. The student's decision to report the incident, supported by Dr. Thompson's advice, reinforced the importance of honesty and accountability.

Promoting Reflective Practice

Encouraging Self-Reflection

Chaplains encourage reflective practice, helping individuals consider their actions and decisions in light of their values. This self-reflection fosters personal growth and ethical development, enabling individuals to align their behavior with their beliefs.

Story: Encouraging Reflective Practice

Rev. Sarah encourages students to engage in regular self-reflection, offering workshops and resources on reflective practices. She helps students explore their values, consider the impact of their actions, and make conscious decisions that align with their ethical beliefs. Her emphasis on reflection promotes continuous personal and ethical growth.

Modeling Ethical Leadership

Leading with Integrity

Chaplains model ethical leadership, demonstrating how to lead with integrity and accountability. Their leadership style emphasizes transparency, respect, and a commitment to ethical principles, providing a blueprint for others to follow.

Case Study: Ethical Leadership in Action

Rabbi Leah's leadership of the university's diversity and inclusion committee exemplifies ethical leadership. She ensures that all voices are heard, decisions are made transparently, and actions are taken with respect and fairness. Her leadership fosters a culture of inclusivity and integrity, inspiring committee members and the broader campus community.

Encouraging Ethical Behavior in Others

Inspiring Positive Change

By modeling ethical behavior, chaplains inspire others to adopt similar standards. Their actions demonstrate the impact of living ethically, encouraging students, faculty, and staff to uphold their values and contribute to a positive campus environment.

Story: Inspiring Ethical Behavior

Imam Rashid's commitment to ethical behavior has inspired many students to take action in their own lives. One student, motivated by Imam Rashid's example, started an ethics club that promotes academic integrity and social responsibility on campus. The club's activities have fostered a greater awareness of ethical issues and encouraged positive change within the student body.

Fostering a Culture of Integrity

Creating an Ethical Environment

Chaplains play a key role in fostering a culture of integrity on campus. By consistently demonstrating ethical behavior and promoting ethical discussions, they create an environment where integrity is valued and upheld.

Case Study: Fostering a Culture of Integrity

Rev. John led a campus-wide initiative to promote academic integrity, collaborating with faculty, administrators, and student leaders. The initiative included workshops, awareness campaigns, and policy changes that emphasized the importance of honesty and accountability. The comprehensive approach helped create a campus culture where academic integrity was respected and maintained.

Supporting Ethical Initiatives

Championing Ethical Projects

Chaplains support and champion ethical initiatives on campus, providing resources, guidance, and encouragement to those involved. Their involvement helps ensure the success of these projects and reinforces the importance of ethical behavior.

Story: Championing a Sustainability Initiative

Dr. Thompson supported a student-led sustainability initiative that aimed to reduce the university's environmental footprint. He provided mentorship, helped secure funding, and promoted the initiative through campus networks. His support was instrumental in the project's success, highlighting the importance of ethical stewardship and environmental responsibility.

Role modeling is a vital aspect of a university chaplain's role in promoting academic and moral integrity. By demonstrating ethical behavior, living out core values, providing guidance, and fostering a culture of integrity, chaplains inspire others to uphold their values and contribute to a positive campus environment. Their actions and interactions serve as a powerful example of how to live ethically and authentically, preparing students to become responsible and ethically-minded leaders in their personal and professional lives.

CHAPTER 08

BUILDING COMMUNITY ON CAMPUS

University chaplains play a crucial role in building a sense of community on campus. By creating a welcoming and inclusive environment, chaplains help foster a sense of belonging among students, faculty, and staff. This chapter explores the various ways chaplains work to build community, including organizing events, creating safe spaces, and promoting inclusivity.

Creating a Welcoming Environment

Organizing Community Events

Bringing People Together

One of the primary ways chaplains build community is by organizing events that bring people together. These events provide opportunities for students, faculty, and staff to connect, share experiences, and celebrate their diversity.

Case Study: Welcome Week Activities

Rev. Sarah organized a series of Welcome Week activities for incoming students, including a community picnic, icebreaker games, and campus tours. These events helped new students feel welcomed and provided opportunities for them to meet their peers, easing their transition into university life.

Celebrating Diversity

Embracing Cultural Differences

Chaplains organize events that celebrate the diverse cultures and traditions represented on campus. These celebrations promote understanding and appreciation of different backgrounds, fostering an inclusive environment.

Story: Cultural Festival

Imam Rashid coordinated a cultural festival that featured music, dance, food, and art from various cultures represented on campus. The festival included performances by student groups, cultural exhibits, and interactive workshops. The event was well-attended and helped students learn about and appreciate each other's cultural heritage.

Creating Safe Spaces

Providing Inclusive Spaces

Chaplains create safe spaces where individuals can express themselves freely and feel supported. These spaces are designed to be inclusive and welcoming to everyone, regardless of their background or beliefs.

Case Study: Multifaith Prayer Room

Rabbi Leah advocated for the establishment of a multifaith prayer room on campus, providing a quiet and inclusive space for students of all faiths to pray, meditate, and reflect. The room was equipped with materials for various religious practices and was open to all members of the campus community. The multifaith prayer room became a valued resource, fostering a sense of inclusion and respect for diverse spiritual practices.

Supporting Marginalized Groups

Offering Targeted Support

Chaplains provide targeted support to marginalized groups on campus, ensuring they have the resources and support they need to thrive. This can include creating support groups, offering counseling, and advocating for their needs.

Story: LGBTQ+ Support Group

Rev. John established an LGBTQ+ support group to provide a safe and supportive space for LGBTQ+ students. The group met regularly to discuss issues, share experiences, and provide mutual support. Rev. John's advocacy and support helped create a more inclusive and accepting environment for LGBTQ+ students on campus.

Promoting Inclusivity

Encouraging Inclusive Practices

Chaplains promote inclusivity by encouraging inclusive practices in all aspects of campus life. This includes working with university administration to develop inclusive policies, providing training on inclusivity, and organizing events that promote diversity and inclusion.

Case Study: Inclusivity Training Workshop

Imam Rashid organized an inclusivity training workshop for faculty and staff, focusing on strategies for creating inclusive classrooms and workplaces. The workshop included presentations, group discussions, and practical exercises. Participants left with a better understanding of how to promote inclusivity and create welcoming environments for all students.

Facilitating Interfaith Dialogue

Encouraging Mutual Understanding

Chaplains facilitate interfaith dialogue, creating opportunities for students of different faiths to share their beliefs and learn from one another. These dialogues promote mutual understanding and respect, helping to build a cohesive and inclusive campus community.

Story: Interfaith Dialogue Series

Rabbi Leah organized an interfaith dialogue series where students from various religious backgrounds came together to discuss their beliefs and practices. The series included guided discussions, panel presentations, and Q&A sessions. The dialogues helped participants develop a deeper understanding of different faiths and fostered a sense of unity and respect.

Building Relationships

Fostering Personal Connections

Chaplains focus on building personal relationships with students, faculty, and staff, providing individualized support, and fostering a sense of community. These relationships help chaplains understand the unique needs and concerns of the campus community and provide tailored support.

Case Study: One-on-One Mentorship

Rev. Sarah offered one-on-one mentorship to students, providing guidance and support on personal, academic, and spiritual matters. Through regular meetings and open communication, she built strong relationships with students, helping them feel connected and supported. Her mentorship fostered a sense of belonging and trust within the campus community.

Encouraging Community Service

Promoting Civic Engagement

Chaplains encourage community service and civic engagement, helping students develop a sense of social responsibility and connection to the broader community. These activities promote teamwork, empathy, and a sense of purpose.

Story: Community Service Day

Imam Rashid organized a Community Service Day, where students, faculty, and staff volunteered at local nonprofit organizations. The event included a variety of service projects, such as cleaning parks, serving meals at shelters, and tutoring children. The day of service fostered a sense of community and demonstrated the positive impact of collective efforts.

Providing Emotional and Spiritual Support

Offering Compassionate Care

Chaplains provide emotional and spiritual support to individuals in need, helping them navigate challenges and find comfort. This support fosters a caring and compassionate campus environment, where everyone feels valued and supported.

Case Study: Emotional Support During Exams

Rabbi Leah recognized the stress students faced during exam periods and organized "Stress Relief Week" activities, including meditation sessions, relaxation workshops, and one-on-one counseling. The activities provided students with tools to manage stress and offered a supportive environment where they could seek help. The initiative helped reduce anxiety and promoted well-being during a challenging time.

Building community on campus is a vital aspect of a university chaplain's role. By creating a welcoming and inclusive environment, organizing events, creating safe spaces, and promoting inclusivity, chaplains help foster a sense of belonging among students, faculty, and staff. Their efforts contribute to a cohesive and supportive campus community, where everyone feels valued and connected. Through their work, chaplains create a positive and inclusive environment that enhances the overall university experience for all members of the campus community.

University chaplains play a crucial role in fostering a sense of community on campus. By organizing events, creating safe spaces, and promoting inclusivity, chaplains help create a welcoming environment where students, faculty, and staff feel a sense of belonging. This chapter focuses on the importance of community service initiatives led by chaplains, which engage the campus community in giving back, providing valuable services to those in need, and strengthening campus bonds.

Community Service

Leading Community Service Initiatives

Inspiring Civic Engagement

Chaplains often take the lead in organizing community service initiatives, inspiring students, faculty, and staff to participate in meaningful projects that benefit the broader community. These initiatives provide opportunities for individuals to develop a sense of social responsibility and engage in civic activities.

Case Study: Annual Day of Service

Rev. John organized an annual Day of Service, bringing together hundreds of students, faculty, and staff to volunteer at various local nonprofits. The day included projects such as cleaning parks, painting community centers, and assisting at food banks. The event fostered a spirit of camaraderie and demonstrated the positive impact of collective efforts in addressing community needs.

Building Connections Through Service

Strengthening Campus Bonds

Community service projects not only benefit external communities but also strengthen the bonds within the campus community. Working together on service projects helps students, faculty, and staff build relationships, develop teamwork skills, and foster a sense of unity and purpose.

Story: Habitat for Humanity Build

Imam Rashid organized a Habitat for Humanity build, where students, faculty, and staff worked together to construct a home for a family in need. The project spanned several weekends and involved tasks such as framing walls, painting, and landscaping. Participants formed strong connections through their shared efforts, and the experience deepened their sense of community and mutual support.

Providing Valuable Services

Addressing Community Needs

Chaplains ensure that community service projects address real needs within the local community. By partnering with local organizations and assessing community needs, chaplains design service initiatives that provide valuable support and resources to those in need.

Case Study: Food Drive for Local Shelter

Rabbi Leah collaborated with a local homeless shelter to organize a campus-wide food drive. She worked with student organizations, residence halls, and faculty departments to collect non-perishable food items. The drive resulted in substantial donations, providing much-needed supplies to the shelter and raising awareness about food insecurity in the local community.

Encouraging Student Leadership

Empowering Future Leaders

Chaplains encourage student leadership in community service initiatives, empowering students to take ownership of projects and develop their leadership skills. This involvement helps students gain confidence, build organizational skills, and foster a lifelong commitment to service.

Story: Student-Led Environmental Cleanup

Rev. Sarah mentored a group of students who wanted to organize an environmental cleanup in the local community. She provided guidance on project planning, fundraising, and volunteer recruitment. The student-led initiative resulted in the removal of several tons of trash from local parks and waterways, and the students gained valuable leadership experience in the process.

Promoting Reflective Practice

Encouraging Reflection and Growth

Chaplains encourage participants to reflect on their community service experiences, helping them connect their actions with their values and personal growth. Reflective practice fosters a deeper understanding of the impact of service and the importance of civic engagement.

Case Study: Reflection Sessions Post-Service

Imam Rashid implemented reflection sessions following community service projects. During these sessions, participants shared their experiences, discussed the challenges they faced, and reflected on the impact of their work. The reflections helped students appreciate the significance of their contributions and reinforced the value of community service.

Creating Long-Term Partnerships

Building Sustainable Relationships

Chaplains work to establish long-term partnerships with local organizations, ensuring that community service initiatives have a lasting impact. These partnerships provide ongoing opportunities for the campus community to engage in meaningful service and support sustainable change.

Story: Long-Term Partnership with a Local School

Rabbi Leah developed a long-term partnership with a local elementary school, where students from the university volunteered as tutors and mentors. The ongoing relationship provided consistent support to the school and enriched the university students' educational experiences. The partnership created a lasting positive impact on both the university and the local community.

Highlighting the Importance of Service

Raising Awareness and Inspiring Action

Chaplains highlight the importance of community service through awareness campaigns, educational programs, and public recognition of volunteers. By raising awareness and celebrating service, chaplains inspire others to get involved and contribute to their communities.

Case Study: Volunteer Recognition Ceremony

Rev. John organized an annual Volunteer Recognition Ceremony to honor students, faculty, and staff who made significant contributions to community service projects. The event included awards, speeches, and presentations about the impact of various initiatives. The ceremony highlighted the importance of service and encouraged continued involvement in community projects.

Addressing Social Justice Issues

Advocating for Change

Chaplains use community service initiatives to address social justice issues, advocating for systemic change and raising awareness about critical social challenges. These initiatives help students understand the broader context of their service work and inspire them to become advocates for justice.

Story: Social Justice Service Project

Imam Rashid led a social justice service project focused on advocating for affordable housing in the local community. The project included volunteering at housing nonprofits, participating in advocacy campaigns, and hosting educational workshops on housing policy. The initiative raised awareness about housing issues and empowered students to take action for social justice.

Community service is a vital aspect of a university chaplain's role in building community on campus. By leading service initiatives, fostering student leadership, and promoting reflective practice, chaplains engage the campus community in meaningful projects that benefit both the university and the broader community. These efforts not only provide valuable services to those in need but also strengthen the bonds within the campus community, fostering a sense of unity, purpose, and social responsibility. Through their work, chaplains create a positive and inclusive environment that enhances the overall university experience for all members of the campus community.

University chaplains play a crucial role in fostering a sense of community on campus. By organizing events, creating safe spaces, and promoting inclusivity, chaplains help create a welcoming environment where students, faculty, and staff feel a sense of belonging. This chapter focuses on how chaplains celebrate the diversity of the campus community by organizing cultural and religious events that highlight different traditions and customs, promoting understanding and appreciation of diversity.

Celebrating Diversity

Organizing Cultural Events

Showcasing Cultural Traditions

Chaplains organize cultural events that showcase the diverse traditions and customs represented on campus. These events provide opportunities for students, faculty, and staff to share their cultural heritage and learn about others, fostering a sense of unity and respect.

Case Study: International Food Festival

Rev. John organized an International Food Festival, where students from various cultural backgrounds prepared and shared traditional dishes from their home countries. The event included music, dance performances, and cultural displays. The festival was a vibrant celebration of diversity, allowing participants to experience and appreciate the rich cultural tapestry of the campus community.

Promoting Intercultural Dialogue

Encouraging Conversations Across Cultures

Cultural events organized by chaplains encourage intercultural dialogue, providing a platform for individuals to engage in meaningful conversations about their traditions and experiences. These dialogues help break down stereotypes and build mutual understanding and respect.

Story: Cultural Storytelling Night

Imam Rashid hosted a Cultural Storytelling Night, where students from different backgrounds shared stories about their cultural traditions and personal experiences. The event included traditional storytelling, poetry readings, and music. Participants left with a deeper appreciation of the diverse cultural narratives within the campus community and the importance of sharing these stories.

Organizing Religious Celebrations

Honoring Diverse Faith Traditions

Chaplains organize religious celebrations that honor the diverse faith traditions on campus. These celebrations provide opportunities for the campus community to learn about and participate in different religious customs, fostering an environment of inclusivity and respect.

Case Study: Multifaith Holiday Celebrations

Rabbi Leah coordinated a series of multifaith holiday celebrations, including Christmas, Hanukkah, Diwali, Eid al-Fitr, and Vesak. Each celebration included educational components, religious rituals, and cultural performances. These events allowed participants to experience and appreciate the significance of various religious holidays, promoting a deeper understanding of the diverse faith traditions on campus.

Facilitating Interfaith Services

Bringing Faith Communities Together

Chaplains facilitate interfaith services that bring together individuals from different religious backgrounds. These services promote a spirit of unity and cooperation, highlighting common values and fostering mutual respect among diverse faith communities.

Story: Interfaith Thanksgiving Service

Rev. Sarah organized an Interfaith Thanksgiving Service, bringing together representatives from various religious traditions to offer prayers of gratitude and reflections on the theme of thanksgiving. The service included readings from sacred texts, music, and a communal meal. Participants from different faith backgrounds expressed their appreciation for the opportunity to come together in a spirit of unity and gratitude.

Educating About Diversity

Providing Educational Programs

Chaplains provide educational programs that promote awareness and understanding of cultural and religious diversity. These programs include workshops, seminars, and guest lectures that address topics such as cultural competence, religious literacy, and the importance of diversity in a global society.

Case Study: Diversity Education Week

Imam Rashid organized a Diversity Education Week, featuring a series of workshops and lectures on topics such as cultural competence, implicit bias, and the benefits of diversity. The week included presentations by experts, interactive activities, and panel discussions. The educational programs helped participants develop a deeper understanding of diversity and its importance in creating an inclusive campus environment.

Collaborating with Cultural and Religious Organizations

Building Partnerships

Chaplains collaborate with cultural and religious organizations on campus to organize events and initiatives that celebrate diversity. These partnerships help ensure that the events are inclusive and representative of the diverse communities on campus.

Story: Partnering with Student Organizations

Rabbi Leah partnered with several student organizations, including the Muslim Student Association, Hindu Student Council, and Black Student Union, to organize a series of cultural and religious events. These partnerships ensured that the events were well-attended and reflective of the diverse interests and traditions of the campus community. The collaborative efforts strengthened relationships between different cultural and religious groups and promoted a spirit of inclusivity.

Creating Inclusive Spaces

Designing Welcoming Environments

Chaplains create inclusive spaces where individuals from diverse backgrounds feel welcomed and respected. These spaces provide a safe environment for cultural and religious expression, fostering a sense of belonging and community.

Case Study: Multicultural Center

Rev. John advocated for the establishment of a Multicultural Center on campus, providing a dedicated space for cultural and religious activities. The center included meeting rooms, a prayer space, and resources for cultural education. The Multicultural Center became a hub for diversity-related events and a welcoming environment for all members of the campus community.

Encouraging Participation and Engagement

Involving the Campus Community

Chaplains encourage active participation and engagement in cultural and religious events, ensuring that these celebrations are accessible and inclusive. By involving the broader campus community, chaplains promote a sense of ownership and investment in celebrating diversity.

Story: Inclusive Event Planning

Imam Rashid involved students, faculty, and staff in the planning and execution of a campus-wide cultural celebration. Committees were formed to handle different aspects of the event, from logistics to programming. The inclusive planning process ensured that the event reflected the diverse interests and traditions of the campus community and encouraged widespread participation.

Highlighting the Importance of Diversity

Raising Awareness and Promoting Inclusion

Chaplains highlight the importance of diversity through awareness campaigns, educational programs, and public recognition of diverse contributions. By raising awareness and celebrating diversity, chaplains inspire others to value and appreciate the richness of the campus community.

Case Study: Diversity Awareness Campaign

Rabbi Leah launched a Diversity Awareness Campaign, featuring posters, social media posts, and informational sessions that highlighted the benefits of diversity and the importance of inclusion. The campaign aimed to educate the campus community about the value of diverse perspectives and foster a more inclusive environment. The initiative was well-received and helped create a greater appreciation for diversity on campus.

Celebrating diversity is a vital aspect of a university chaplain's role in building community on campus. By organizing cultural and religious events, promoting intercultural dialogue, and providing educational programs, chaplains help foster understanding and appreciation of the diverse traditions and customs represented within the campus community. Their efforts contribute to a cohesive and inclusive environment where everyone feels valued and respected. Through their work, chaplains create a positive and enriching university experience for all members of the campus community.

CHAPTER 09

THE CHAPLAIN'S INVOLVEMENT IN CAMPUS EVENTS

University chaplains play a significant role in campus events, providing spiritual support and adding a meaningful dimension to various academic ceremonies and gatherings. Their involvement enriches these events, fostering a sense of community and reflection. This chapter explores the various ways chaplains contribute to academic ceremonies such as convocations, graduations, and memorial services.

Academic Ceremonies

Convocations

Opening the Academic Year

Convocations mark the beginning of the academic year, welcoming new students and setting the tone for the months ahead. Chaplains are often invited to offer prayers, blessings, and reflections that inspire and motivate the campus community.

Case Study: Convocation Prayer

Rev. John was invited to deliver the invocation at the university's annual convocation. He offered a prayer that emphasized the importance of learning, community, and personal growth. His words resonated with the audience, creating a reflective and hopeful atmosphere for the new academic year.

Blessings and Reflections

Inspiring the Community

Chaplains provide blessings and reflections during convocations, offering words of wisdom and encouragement. These contributions highlight the spiritual dimension of the academic journey and inspire students, faculty, and staff to pursue excellence and integrity.

Story: Convocation Reflection

Imam Rashid delivered a reflection at the convocation ceremony, focusing on the theme of resilience and perseverance. He shared stories of overcoming challenges and encouraged students to remain steadfast in their academic pursuits. His reflection provided a sense of encouragement and purpose, setting a positive tone for the academic year.

Graduations

Celebrating Achievements

Graduation ceremonies are significant milestones in the academic journey, marking the culmination of years of hard work and dedication. Chaplains play a crucial role in these ceremonies, offering prayers, blessings, and reflections that honor the achievements of graduates and provide a sense of closure and new beginnings.

Case Study: Graduation Invocation

Rabbi Leah was asked to deliver the invocation at the university's graduation ceremony. She offered a prayer of gratitude for the graduates' accomplishments and blessings for their future endeavors. Her words added a spiritual dimension to the celebration, acknowledging the significance of the moment and the potential of the graduates' futures.

Offering Blessings

Honoring Graduates

Chaplains offer blessings during graduation ceremonies, recognizing the achievements of graduates and wishing them success in their future endeavors. These blessings provide a sense of spiritual support and encouragement as graduates transition to the next phase of their lives.

Story: Graduation Blessing

Rev. Sarah gave a blessing at the commencement ceremony, celebrating the graduates' hard work and dedication. She invoked blessings for their future journeys, encouraging them to use their knowledge and skills to make a positive impact in the world. Her heartfelt words resonated with graduates and their families, adding depth to the celebration.

Memorial Services

Honoring Lives and Legacies

Memorial services on campus provide an opportunity to honor and remember members of the university community who have passed away. Chaplains play a central role in these services, offering prayers, reflections, and support to those in mourning.

Case Study: Memorial Service for a Faculty Member

Dr. Thompson organized a memorial service for a beloved faculty member who had passed away. The service included tributes from colleagues and students, music, and a reflection by Dr. Thompson. His words of comfort and remembrance helped the community come together to honor the faculty member's life and legacy.

Providing Comfort and Support

Offering Spiritual Guidance

Chaplains provide comfort and support during memorial services, offering prayers and reflections that help the community process their grief and find solace. Their presence and words offer spiritual guidance and reassurance during difficult times.

Story: Reflection at a Memorial Service

Imam Rashid offered a reflection at a memorial service for a student who had passed away unexpectedly. He spoke about the importance of community, remembrance, and finding strength in faith. His words provided comfort to the grieving family and friends, helping them navigate their sorrow and honor the student's memory.

Other Campus Events

Participating in Diverse Gatherings

Chaplains are involved in a wide range of campus events beyond academic ceremonies, including lectures, panel discussions, cultural celebrations, and community service projects. Their participation enriches these events, adding a spiritual and ethical perspective.

Case Study: Interfaith Panel Discussion

Rabbi Leah participated in an interfaith panel discussion on the topic of faith and social justice. She shared insights from her religious tradition and engaged in meaningful dialogue with representatives from other faiths.

Her contributions helped foster a deeper understanding of the intersection between faith and social justice, enriching the conversation and promoting interfaith collaboration.

Fostering a Sense of Community

Building Connections

By participating in various campus events, chaplains help build connections within the university community. Their presence and engagement foster a sense of belonging and mutual respect, contributing to a positive and inclusive campus culture.

Story: Cultural Celebration Participation

Rev. Sarah actively participated in a campus cultural celebration, joining in the festivities and offering a blessing for the event. Her involvement demonstrated the chaplaincy's commitment to celebrating diversity and building an inclusive community. Her presence was appreciated by students, faculty, and staff, enhancing the sense of unity and celebration.

Chaplains play a significant role in academic ceremonies and other campus events, offering prayers, blessings, and reflections that add a spiritual dimension to these important gatherings. Their involvement enriches the campus community, fostering a sense of belonging, reflection, and mutual respect. Through their participation in convocations, graduations, memorial services, and other events, chaplains contribute to the holistic experience of university life, supporting the spiritual and emotional well-being of students, faculty, and staff.

University chaplains play a significant role in campus events, providing spiritual support and adding a meaningful dimension to various academic ceremonies and gatherings. Their involvement enriches these events, fostering a sense of community and reflection. This chapter explores how chaplains support and participate in student-led activities, such as club meetings, service projects, and social events, demonstrating their commitment to student life and well-being.

Student-Led Activities

Supporting Club Meetings

Providing Guidance and Encouragement

Chaplains support a wide range of student clubs and organizations, offering guidance and encouragement. Their involvement helps ensure that these groups operate with a sense of purpose and integrity, fostering an inclusive and supportive environment.

Case Study: Faith-Based Club Meeting

Rev. John regularly attended meetings of a faith-based student club, providing spiritual guidance and support. He helped the club plan activities, lead discussions on religious topics, and offer prayers. His presence reassured the students that their spiritual growth and community were valued by the university.

Promoting Interfaith Clubs

Encouraging Collaboration

Chaplains promote the formation and growth of interfaith clubs, encouraging collaboration among students from diverse religious backgrounds. These clubs provide a platform for interfaith dialogue, mutual understanding, and joint initiatives.

Story: Interfaith Club Collaboration

Imam Rashid supported the creation of an interfaith club that brought together students from various religious traditions. He facilitated initial meetings, helped plan events, and provided resources on interfaith dialogue. The club organized activities such as interfaith discussions, service projects, and cultural celebrations, fostering a spirit of unity and respect among its members.

Participating in Service Projects

Leading by Example

Chaplains actively participate in student-led service projects, leading by example and demonstrating the importance of giving back to the community. Their involvement inspires students to engage in civic activities and develop a sense of social responsibility.

Case Study: Habitat for Humanity Build

Rabbi Leah joined students in a Habitat for Humanity build, working alongside them to construct a home for a family in need. She provided guidance, encouragement, and a spiritual perspective on the importance of service. Her participation motivated students to contribute their time and effort, fostering a sense of accomplishment and community.

Supporting Ongoing Initiatives

Ensuring Sustainability

Chaplains help ensure the sustainability of student-led service initiatives by providing ongoing support and mentorship. They assist with project planning, fundraising, and volunteer recruitment, helping students navigate challenges and achieve their goals.

Story: Long-Term Mentorship for a Service Initiative

Rev. Sarah mentored a group of students who organized a long-term service initiative focused on tutoring children in underserved communities. She provided guidance on logistics, secured funding, and helped recruit volunteers. Her ongoing support helped the initiative grow and succeed, positively impacting both the students and the children they served.

Participating in Social Events

Building Community Through Engagement

Chaplains participate in student-led social events, contributing to the sense of community and belonging on campus. Their presence at these events demonstrates their commitment to student life and helps build relationships in a relaxed and informal setting.

Case Study: Student Talent Show

Imam Rashid attended a student talent show, supporting participants and engaging with the audience. He offered words of encouragement and appreciation for the students' talents and efforts. His presence added a sense of warmth and community to the event, reinforcing the importance of celebrating student achievements.

Encouraging Inclusive Social Activities

Promoting Diversity and Inclusion

Chaplains encourage inclusive social activities that welcome all students, regardless of their background or beliefs. They help plan and support events that celebrate diversity and foster a sense of belonging for everyone.

Story: Inclusive Social Event Planning

Rabbi Leah helped plan a campus-wide social event that included activities representing different cultures and traditions. The event featured international cuisine, music, and dance performances, as well as interactive workshops on cultural practices. Her involvement ensured that the event was inclusive and reflective of the diverse student body, fostering a sense of unity and respect.

Providing Emotional and Spiritual Support

Being Available to Students

Chaplains make themselves available to students during social events, offering emotional and spiritual support as needed. Their presence provides a reassuring and supportive environment where students can seek guidance and comfort.

Case Study: Emotional Support at a Campus Festival

Rev. John attended a campus festival where he made himself available to students who needed someone to talk to. Throughout the event, he engaged with students, listened to their concerns, and offered words of encouragement and support. His approachable demeanor and willingness to be present provided a valuable resource for students navigating personal challenges.

Encouraging Student Leadership

Empowering Students to Lead

Chaplains encourage and empower students to take on leadership roles in organizing and executing activities. By providing mentorship and support, chaplains help students develop essential leadership skills and confidence.

Story: Student Leadership Development

Imam Rashid worked closely with a group of students planning a large-scale charity event. He provided mentorship on event planning, fundraising, and volunteer management, encouraging the students to take ownership of the project. The students successfully organized the event, raising significant funds for a local charity and gaining valuable leadership experience.

Celebrating Student Achievements

Recognizing and Honoring Efforts

Chaplains celebrate student achievements by recognizing and honoring their efforts in various activities. This acknowledgment reinforces the importance of their contributions and encourages continued engagement and excellence.

Case Study: Recognition Ceremony for Volunteers

Rabbi Leah organized a recognition ceremony for students who had volunteered their time and efforts in various service projects throughout the year. The ceremony included awards, speeches, and a celebration of the students' contributions. The event highlighted the positive impact of their work and encouraged ongoing commitment to service and community engagement.

Supporting and participating in student-led activities is a vital aspect of a university chaplain's role in building community on campus. By engaging in club meetings, service projects, and social events, chaplains demonstrate their commitment to student life and well-being. Their presence and involvement foster a sense of belonging, encourage student leadership, and promote a supportive and inclusive campus environment. Through their efforts, chaplains contribute to a positive and enriching university experience for all members of the campus community.

University chaplains play a significant role in campus events, providing spiritual support and adding a meaningful dimension to various academic ceremonies and gatherings. Their involvement enriches these events, fostering a sense of community and reflection. This chapter explores how chaplains help maintain and enrich university traditions by incorporating spiritual elements and encouraging participation, thus creating a sense of continuity and community on campus.

University Traditions

Incorporating Spiritual Elements

Enriching Traditions with Spiritual Depth

Chaplains play a key role in incorporating spiritual elements into university traditions. By offering prayers, reflections, and blessings, they add depth and meaning to these traditions, making them more inclusive and reflective of the diverse campus community.

Case Study: Founders Day Celebration

Rev. John was invited to deliver an invocation at the university's annual Founders Day celebration. He offered a prayer that honored the institution's history and legacy, invoking blessings for its future. His words connected the community to the university's roots while inspiring hope and commitment to its continued growth and success.

Promoting Participation

Encouraging Engagement in Traditions

Chaplains encourage students, faculty, and staff to actively participate in university traditions. By fostering a sense of belonging and ownership, they help ensure that these traditions are vibrant and well-attended, strengthening the campus community.

Story: Homecoming Weekend

Imam Rashid played a significant role in promoting participation in the university's Homecoming Weekend. He engaged with student organizations, faculty, and alumni to plan events and encourage involvement. His efforts led to a highly successful weekend that celebrated school spirit and brought together the entire campus community.

Maintaining Continuity

Preserving and Evolving Traditions

Chaplains help maintain the continuity of university traditions, ensuring that they are preserved while also evolving to reflect the changing campus community. This balance of preservation and innovation helps traditions remain relevant and meaningful.

Case Study: Candlelight Vigil

Rabbi Leah was instrumental in organizing the annual candlelight vigil, a tradition that honors the memory of students, faculty, and staff who have passed away. She ensured that the vigil maintained its solemn and reflective nature while incorporating new elements, such as interfaith prayers and student-led reflections, to make it more inclusive and impactful.

Creating New Traditions

Innovating with Purpose

Chaplains are often at the forefront of creating new traditions that address emerging needs and reflect the evolving values of the university community. These new traditions help build a sense of unity and shared purpose.

Story: Environmental Sustainability Day

Rev. Sarah initiated a new tradition, Environmental Sustainability Day, to raise awareness about environmental issues and promote sustainable practices on campus. The day included educational workshops, a campus clean-up, and a tree-planting ceremony. This new tradition quickly became an important part of the university calendar, reflecting the community's commitment to environmental stewardship.

Supporting Legacy Events

Enhancing Established Traditions

Chaplains support and enhance established university traditions by adding their unique spiritual and ethical perspectives. Their involvement helps these events resonate more deeply with participants and reinforces their significance.

Case Study: Commencement Ceremonies

Dr. Thompson regularly participates in the university's commencement ceremonies, offering invocations and blessings that honor the achievements of graduates and inspire them as they embark on their future endeavors. His heartfelt contributions enhance the ceremony's emotional and spiritual resonance, making it a memorable and meaningful experience for graduates and their families.

Fostering Community Through Traditions

Building a Sense of Belonging

University traditions play a crucial role in building a sense of belonging and community. Chaplains help foster this sense of belonging by ensuring that traditions are inclusive and accessible to all members of the campus community.

Story: Inclusive Holiday Celebrations

Imam Rashid collaborated with various student groups to organize inclusive holiday celebrations that reflected the diverse religious and cultural backgrounds of the campus community. These celebrations included Christmas, Hanukkah, Kwanzaa, Diwali, and Eid al-Fitr, among others. By promoting and participating in these events, he helped create a welcoming and inclusive environment where everyone felt valued and respected.

Promoting Intergenerational Connections

Bridging Generations

Chaplains help bridge generations by promoting traditions that connect current students with alumni and faculty. These intergenerational connections strengthen the sense of continuity and shared identity within the university community.

Case Study: Alumni Mentorship Program

Rev. John supported the establishment of an alumni mentorship program that connected current students with alumni mentors. The program included an annual mentorship dinner, where students and alumni could share experiences and build lasting relationships. This tradition helped foster a sense of continuity and mutual support across generations.

Highlighting Core Values

Reinforcing Institutional Values

Through their involvement in university traditions, chaplains highlight and reinforce the core values of the institution. Their contributions help ensure that these values are celebrated and upheld, fostering a culture of integrity, respect, and community.

Story: Honor Code Signing Ceremony

Rabbi Leah played a key role in the annual Honor Code Signing Ceremony, where incoming students pledged to uphold the university's values of honesty, respect, and academic integrity. She offered a reflection on the importance of these values and their impact on personal and academic life. Her words reinforced the significance of the Honor Code and inspired students to commit to living by these principles.

Celebrating Milestones

Marking Significant Achievements

Chaplains participate in ceremonies that celebrate significant milestones in the academic journey, such as awards banquets, research showcases, and leadership recognitions. Their involvement adds a spiritual and ethical dimension to these celebrations, honoring the achievements of individuals and the community.

Case Study: Research Excellence Awards

Dr. Thompson was invited to offer a blessing at the university's Research Excellence Awards ceremony. He spoke about the pursuit of knowledge and the importance of using research to benefit society. His reflection added depth to the celebration, highlighting the ethical responsibilities that come with academic achievement.

Chaplains play a vital role in maintaining and enriching university traditions. By incorporating spiritual elements, promoting participation, and creating new traditions, they help build a sense of continuity and community on campus. Their involvement in academic ceremonies, legacy events, and milestone celebrations adds depth and meaning, fostering a culture of inclusivity, respect, and shared purpose. Through their efforts, chaplains contribute to a vibrant and cohesive university community that values its traditions while embracing growth and change.

CHAPTER 10

NAVIGATING ETHICAL DILEMMAS

University chaplains often face complex ethical dilemmas that require them to balance their personal beliefs with their professional responsibilities. Navigating these challenges involves a careful consideration of religious teachings, university policies, and the diverse needs of the campus community. This chapter explores how chaplains manage these ethical dilemmas, offering insights and strategies for maintaining integrity and professionalism.

Balancing Beliefs and Responsibilities

Understanding the Role of a Chaplain

Defining Professional Boundaries

Chaplains must clearly understand their role within the university, recognizing the boundaries between their personal beliefs and their professional responsibilities. This understanding helps them navigate situations where conflicts may arise, ensuring they provide equitable support to all students, regardless of their background or beliefs.

Case Study: Respecting Diverse Beliefs

Rev. John was approached by a student seeking guidance on a matter that conflicted with his personal religious beliefs. Understanding his professional role, Rev. John focused on providing support that respected the student's autonomy and diverse perspectives, ensuring his personal beliefs did not interfere with his professional responsibilities.

Navigating Conflicts Between Teachings and Policies

Aligning with Institutional Values

Chaplains often encounter conflicts between religious teachings and university policies. In such cases, they must find ways to uphold their faith while respecting the institution's values and regulations. This balance requires a nuanced understanding of both realms and a commitment to ethical practice.

Story: Addressing Policy Conflicts

Imam Rashid faced a situation where a university policy on inclusivity conflicted with certain interpretations of religious teachings. He sought guidance from his religious community and engaged in dialogue with university leadership to find a solution that respected both the policy and his faith. This collaborative approach helped him navigate the dilemma while maintaining his professional integrity.

Providing Inclusive Support

Ensuring Fairness and Equity

Chaplains are tasked with providing support that is inclusive and equitable, regardless of their personal beliefs. This involves creating an environment where all students feel valued and respected, and ensuring that their services are accessible to everyone.

Case Study: Inclusive Counseling Practices

Rabbi Leah worked with students from various religious and cultural backgrounds, ensuring her counseling practices were inclusive and respectful. She participated in cultural competency training and sought feedback from students to improve her approach, demonstrating her commitment to providing fair and equitable support.

Handling Sensitive Topics

Approaching Controversial Issues

Chaplains often deal with sensitive and controversial topics, such as sexuality, gender identity, and reproductive rights. Navigating these discussions requires sensitivity, openness, and a commitment to supporting students without imposing personal beliefs.

Story: Navigating Controversial Discussions

Rev. Sarah was asked to facilitate a discussion on gender identity and sexuality. Aware of the diverse beliefs within the campus community, she created a respectful and inclusive environment for the discussion. She encouraged open dialogue and ensured that all voices were heard, fostering a space where students felt safe to express their views and experiences.

Seeking Guidance and Support

Consulting with Peers and Mentors

When faced with ethical dilemmas, chaplains benefit from seeking guidance and support from their peers, mentors, and professional networks. This collaboration provides different perspectives and helps them navigate complex situations with greater clarity.

Case Study: Peer Support Network

Dr. Thompson regularly participated in a peer support network of chaplains from various institutions. This group provided a confidential space to discuss ethical dilemmas and seek advice. The collective wisdom and diverse perspectives of his peers helped Dr. Thompson navigate challenging situations more effectively.

Developing Ethical Frameworks

Creating Guidelines for Practice

Chaplains can benefit from developing ethical frameworks and guidelines that inform their practice. These frameworks help them approach dilemmas systematically and consistently, ensuring their actions align with both their professional responsibilities and personal integrity.

Story: Establishing Ethical Guidelines

Imam Rashid, in collaboration with other chaplains and university administrators, developed a set of ethical guidelines for the chaplaincy program. These guidelines outlined principles for handling conflicts, providing inclusive support, and maintaining professional boundaries. The guidelines served as a valuable resource for navigating ethical dilemmas and promoting consistent practice.

Reflecting on Personal Beliefs

Engaging in Self-Reflection

Regular self-reflection helps chaplains understand their personal beliefs and how these beliefs influence their professional practice. By examining their values and biases, chaplains can better navigate ethical dilemmas and provide balanced support.

Case Study: Personal Reflection Practice

Rabbi Leah engaged in regular self-reflection, journaling about her experiences and challenges as a chaplain. This practice helped her identify areas where her personal beliefs might impact her professional responsibilities, allowing her to address potential conflicts proactively and ensure her support remained fair and inclusive.

Engaging in Continuous Learning

Staying Informed and Updated

Chaplains must stay informed about developments in both their religious traditions and the broader context of higher education. Continuous learning helps them navigate ethical dilemmas with an informed perspective and adapt to changing circumstances.

Story: Continuous Professional Development

Rev. John participated in ongoing professional development opportunities, including workshops on ethical decision-making, diversity and inclusion, and mental health support. This commitment to continuous learning helped him stay updated on best practices and navigate ethical dilemmas more effectively.

Promoting Open Dialogue

Encouraging Communication and Understanding

Open dialogue with students, faculty, and staff helps chaplains understand different perspectives and build trust. By promoting communication and understanding, chaplains can navigate ethical dilemmas more effectively and foster a supportive campus environment.

Case Study: Open Dialogue Forums

Dr. Thompson organized regular open dialogue forums where students could discuss ethical and spiritual issues. These forums provided a platform for sharing diverse viewpoints and promoting mutual understanding. The open communication fostered by these forums helped Dr. Thompson address ethical dilemmas with greater insight and sensitivity.

Navigating ethical dilemmas is a complex and essential aspect of a university chaplain's role. By balancing their personal beliefs with their professional responsibilities, chaplains ensure they provide inclusive and equitable support to all members of the campus community. Through understanding their role, seeking guidance, engaging in self-reflection, and promoting open dialogue, chaplains can navigate ethical challenges with integrity and professionalism. Their ability to manage these dilemmas contributes to a respectful and inclusive campus environment, fostering trust and support among students, faculty, and staff.

University chaplains often face complex ethical dilemmas that require them to balance their personal beliefs with their professional responsibilities. Navigating these challenges involves a careful consideration of religious teachings, university policies, and the diverse needs of the campus community. This chapter explores how chaplains manage these ethical dilemmas, particularly focusing on maintaining confidentiality and trust, which are crucial aspects of their role.

Confidentiality and Trust

The Importance of Confidentiality

Building a Foundation of Trust

Confidentiality is a cornerstone of a chaplain's relationship with students, faculty, and staff. By maintaining confidentiality, chaplains build a foundation of trust, which is essential for providing effective support and guidance.

Case Study: Confidential Counseling Session

Rev. John was approached by a student dealing with severe anxiety and personal issues. He assured the student that their conversation would remain confidential, which encouraged the student to speak openly. This trust allowed Rev. John to provide meaningful support and guidance, helping the student navigate their challenges.

Navigating Confidentiality and Disclosure

Understanding When to Intervene

Chaplains must navigate the tension between maintaining confidentiality and recognizing situations where disclosure is necessary to protect individuals or the campus community. This requires a clear understanding of legal and ethical guidelines regarding confidentiality and mandatory reporting.

Story: Balancing Confidentiality and Safety

Imam Rashid was counseling a student who expressed suicidal thoughts. While maintaining confidentiality was crucial, the immediate risk to the student's safety required intervention. Imam Rashid carefully explained the need to involve mental health professionals and ensured the students received the necessary support while respecting their privacy as much as possible.

Establishing Confidentiality Protocols

Creating Clear Guidelines

Chaplains benefit from establishing clear confidentiality protocols that outline how they will handle sensitive information. These protocols help chaplains navigate ethical dilemmas and provide consistent support.

Case Study: Developing Confidentiality Guidelines

Rabbi Leah, in collaboration with university administrators, developed confidentiality guidelines for the chaplaincy program. These guidelines included protocols for maintaining confidentiality, circumstances that necessitate disclosure, and procedures for obtaining consent. The guidelines provided a framework for handling sensitive information ethically and responsibly.

Communicating Confidentiality Limits

Setting Expectations with Students

Chaplains must communicate the limits of confidentiality to students, faculty, and staff, ensuring they understand when information may need to be disclosed. This transparency helps manage expectations and maintains trust.

Story: Explaining Confidentiality Boundaries

Rev. Sarah met with a student who was struggling with substance abuse. At the beginning of their conversation, she explained the limits of confidentiality, including situations where she might need to disclose information to protect the student's safety. This clarity helped the students feel informed and secure in their discussions with Rev. Sarah.

Balancing Privacy and Intervention

Making Ethical Decisions

Chaplains often face difficult decisions when balancing privacy and the need for intervention. These decisions require careful consideration of the potential harm and the ethical implications of disclosure.

Case Study: Ethical Decision-Making Process

Dr. Thompson encountered a situation where a student confided in him about being in an abusive relationship. While maintaining confidentiality was important, the immediate risk to the student's safety required action. Dr.

Thompson consulted with mental health professionals and followed university protocols to ensure the student received support while carefully handling the sensitive information.

Seeking Guidance and Support

Consulting with Peers and Experts

When faced with challenging confidentiality issues, chaplains benefit from seeking guidance from peers, mentors, and legal experts. This support helps them navigate ethical dilemmas and make informed decisions.

Story: Peer Consultation for Ethical Dilemmas

Imam Rashid participated in a peer consultation group with other chaplains, where they discussed complex confidentiality cases. This collaborative approach provided diverse perspectives and helped him navigate difficult situations more effectively, ensuring he maintained ethical standards while addressing students' needs.

Engaging in Continuous Learning

Staying Informed on Legal and Ethical Standards

Chaplains must stay informed about legal and ethical standards related to confidentiality and mandatory reporting. Continuous learning helps them navigate ethical dilemmas with up-to-date knowledge and best practices.

Case Study: Professional Development in Confidentiality

Rev. John attended a professional development workshop on confidentiality and ethical decision-making. The workshop covered recent legal updates, case studies, and best practices for maintaining confidentiality while addressing safety concerns. This training enhanced his ability to handle sensitive information responsibly and ethically.

Promoting a Culture of Trust

Fostering Open Communication

Chaplains play a crucial role in promoting a culture of trust within the campus community. By fostering open communication and demonstrating their commitment to confidentiality, chaplains help create a supportive environment where individuals feel safe to seek guidance.

Story: Building a Trusting Environment

Rabbi Leah worked diligently to create an environment of trust within the university's counseling center. She consistently demonstrated her commitment to confidentiality and respect for privacy, which encouraged more students to seek her support. Her efforts contributed to a campus culture where individuals felt secure in discussing their concerns and receiving help.

Reflecting on Personal Beliefs

Engaging in Self-Reflection

Regular self-reflection helps chaplains understand their personal beliefs and how these beliefs influence their professional practice. By examining their values and biases, chaplains can better navigate ethical dilemmas related to confidentiality and trust.

Case Study: Personal Reflection Practice

Rev. Sarah engaged in regular self-reflection, journaling about her experiences and challenges as a chaplain. This practice helped her identify areas where her personal beliefs might impact her professional responsibilities, allowing her to address potential conflicts proactively and ensure her support remained fair and inclusive.

Maintaining confidentiality and trust is a critical aspect of a chaplain's role. By balancing the need for privacy with the necessity of intervention in certain situations, chaplains ensure they provide ethical and effective support to all members of the campus community. Through establishing clear guidelines, communicating limits, seeking guidance, and promoting a culture of trust, chaplains navigate these ethical dilemmas with integrity and professionalism. Their ability to manage these challenges contributes to a respectful and inclusive campus environment, fostering trust and support among students, faculty, and staff.

University chaplains often face complex ethical dilemmas that require them to balance their personal beliefs with their professional responsibilities. Navigating these challenges involves careful consideration of religious teachings, university policies, and the diverse needs of the campus community. This chapter explores how chaplains strive to make inclusive and ethical decisions that respect the diverse beliefs and values of the campus community, often involving seeking input from multiple perspectives.

Inclusive Decision-Making

Embracing Diversity in Decision-Making

Understanding the Importance of Inclusivity

Chaplains recognize the importance of making decisions that reflect and respect the diverse beliefs and values within the campus community. Inclusive decision-making ensures that all voices are heard and considered, promoting a sense of belonging and respect.

Case Study: Planning an Interfaith Event

Rev. John was tasked with organizing an interfaith event on campus. To ensure the event was inclusive, he consulted with representatives from various religious and cultural groups. By incorporating their input, he created a program that honored multiple traditions and fostered mutual understanding and respect among participants.

Seeking Multiple Perspectives

Encouraging Diverse Input

Inclusive decision-making involves seeking input from a wide range of perspectives. Chaplains actively engage with different groups on campus to understand their views and incorporate their feedback into decisions.

Story: Student Advisory Council

Imam Rashid established a Student Advisory Council composed of representatives from various student organizations, including faith-based, cultural, and advocacy groups. The council met regularly to discuss campus issues and provide input on decisions affecting the community. This collaborative approach ensured that decisions reflected the diverse needs and values of the student body.

Balancing Competing Interests

Navigating Conflicting Needs

Chaplains often face situations where the needs and values of different groups conflict. Inclusive decision-making requires balancing these competing interests with sensitivity and fairness, finding solutions that respect all parties involved.

Case Study: Scheduling Events During Religious Holidays

Rabbi Leah encountered a scheduling conflict when planning a major campus event that coincided with a significant religious holiday. She consulted with affected groups and found an alternative date that accommodated everyone's needs. This decision demonstrated her commitment to inclusivity and respect for diverse religious practices.

Creating Inclusive Policies

Developing Guidelines That Reflect Diversity

Chaplains contribute to developing campus policies and guidelines that reflect the diverse beliefs and values of the community. These inclusive policies promote equity and ensure that all members of the campus community feel respected and valued.

Story: Inclusive Housing Policy

Rev. Sarah worked with university administrators to develop an inclusive housing policy that accommodated the needs of students from various religious and cultural backgrounds. The policy included provisions for gender-neutral housing, dietary accommodations, and spaces for religious practices. Her involvement ensured that the policy was comprehensive and respectful of diversity.

Promoting Open Dialogue

Facilitating Constructive Conversations

Inclusive decision-making is supported by open dialogue and constructive conversations. Chaplains facilitate discussions where all voices can be heard, fostering an environment of mutual respect and understanding.

Case Study: Campus-Wide Forums

Dr. Thompson organized campus-wide forums to discuss important issues and gather input from the community. These forums provided a platform for students, faculty, and staff to share their perspectives and contribute to decision-making processes. The open dialogue helped build consensus and ensure that decisions were informed by diverse viewpoints.

Engaging in Ethical Reflection

Considering Ethical Implications

Chaplains engage in ethical reflection when making decisions, considering the potential impact on the campus community. This reflection helps ensure that decisions are aligned with the university's values and ethical standards.

Story: Reflective Decision-Making Process

Imam Rashid faced a difficult decision regarding the allocation of limited resources for student programs. He took time to reflect on the ethical implications, consulted with colleagues and sought input from affected groups. This reflective process helped him make a decision that was fair, transparent, and ethically sound.

Building Consensus

Striving for Agreement

Inclusive decision-making often involves building consensus among diverse stakeholders. Chaplains work to find common ground and develop solutions that are acceptable to all parties, fostering a sense of collective ownership and commitment.

Case Study: Consensus-Building in Program Development

Rabbi Leah led a committee to develop a new wellness program for students. The committee included representatives from various campus groups, and decisions were made through consensus-building. This collaborative approach ensured that the program addressed the needs and values of the entire campus community and garnered widespread support.

Training and Education

Promoting Inclusivity Through Learning

Chaplains promote inclusivity by providing training and education on inclusive practices and decision-making. These programs help the campus community understand the importance of diversity and develop skills for making inclusive decisions.

Story: Inclusivity Training Workshops

Rev. John organized a series of inclusivity training workshops for faculty, staff, and student leaders. The workshops covered topics such as cultural competency, unconscious bias, and inclusive decision-making. Participants gained valuable insights and tools for promoting inclusivity in their roles, enhancing the overall campus culture.

Evaluating Decisions and Outcomes

Assessing Impact and Making Adjustments

Chaplains evaluate the impact of their decisions and seek feedback to ensure they meet the needs of the campus community. This ongoing assessment allows them to make adjustments and continuously improve their inclusive practices.

Case Study: Feedback and Improvement

Dr. Thompson implemented a new mentorship program and sought feedback from participants after the first semester. Based on the feedback, he made adjustments to improve the program's inclusivity and effectiveness. This commitment to evaluation and improvement demonstrated his dedication to meeting the diverse needs of the community.

Inclusive decision-making is a critical aspect of a university chaplain's role. By seeking input from diverse perspectives, balancing competing interests, and promoting open dialogue, chaplains ensure that their decisions respect and reflect the diverse beliefs and values of the campus community. Engaging in ethical reflection, building consensus, and providing training and education further support their efforts to make inclusive and ethical decisions. Through these practices, chaplains contribute to a respectful, inclusive, and cohesive campus environment, fostering trust and support among students, faculty, and staff.

CHAPTER 11

THE FUTURE OF CAMPUS MINISTRY

The role of university chaplains is continually evolving in response to changes in higher education and society. Chaplains must adapt to new challenges and opportunities, such as the increasing diversity of student populations and the rise of digital technology. This chapter explores the future of campus ministry, focusing on how chaplains can adapt to these changes while continuing to provide meaningful support to the campus community.

Adapting to Change

Embracing Diversity

Responding to Increasing Diversity

The increasing diversity of student populations requires chaplains to develop new strategies and approaches to support a wide range of beliefs, cultures, and backgrounds.

Embracing this diversity enriches the campus community and enhances the chaplaincy's relevance.

Case Study: Cultural Competency Training

Rev. John implemented cultural competency training for the chaplaincy team, focusing on understanding and respecting the diverse backgrounds of students. The training included workshops on cultural sensitivity, bias awareness, and effective communication. This initiative improved the team's ability to provide inclusive support and fostered a more welcoming environment for all students.

Promoting Interfaith Dialogue

Encouraging Mutual Understanding

As campuses become more diverse, promoting interfaith dialogue becomes increasingly important. Chaplains can facilitate conversations that encourage mutual understanding and respect among students from different religious and cultural backgrounds.

Story: Interfaith Dialogue Series

Imam Rashid organized an interfaith dialogue series, bringing together students from various religious traditions to discuss their beliefs and practices. The series included panel discussions, Q&A sessions, and small group discussions. This initiative helped students develop a deeper understanding of different faiths and fostered a sense of unity and respect on campus.

Leveraging Digital Technology

Embracing Digital Tools

The rise of digital technology presents both challenges and opportunities for campus ministry. Chaplains can leverage digital tools to enhance their outreach, provide virtual support, and create online communities that extend their reach beyond the physical campus.

Case Study: Virtual Support Sessions

Rabbi Leah introduced virtual support sessions for students who were unable to attend in-person meetings due to distance or scheduling conflicts. Using video conferencing tools, she provided counseling, spiritual direction, and group discussions. This approach allowed her to support a broader range of students and adapt to their needs in a flexible manner.

Creating Online Communities

Building Virtual Connections

Chaplains can create online communities that provide a platform for students to connect, share experiences, and support one another. These virtual spaces complement in-person interactions and ensure that students can access support regardless of their location.

Story: Online Spiritual Community

Rev. Sarah established an online spiritual community using social media and a dedicated website. The community featured discussion forums, virtual prayer meetings, and resources on various spiritual topics. This initiative allowed students to engage with their faith and connect with others in a digital environment, enhancing their sense of belonging and support.

Addressing Mental Health

Integrating Mental Health Support

The growing awareness of mental health issues on campus requires chaplains to integrate mental health support into their services. By collaborating with counseling centers and offering specialized training, chaplains can provide comprehensive support that addresses both spiritual and emotional well-being.

Case Study: Mental Health First Aid Training

Dr. Thompson participated in Mental Health First Aid training to better support students experiencing mental health crises. The training equipped him with skills to recognize signs of mental distress, provide initial support, and refer students to professional resources. This proactive approach enhanced the chaplaincy's ability to address the holistic needs of students.

Collaborating with Campus Partners

Strengthening Campus Partnerships

Chaplains can strengthen their impact by collaborating with other campus departments, such as student affairs, academic advising, and diversity and inclusion offices. These partnerships enhance the chaplaincy's ability to support students and address complex issues.

Story: Collaboration with Diversity Office

Imam Rashid collaborated with the university's diversity and inclusion office to develop programs that addressed issues of equity and social justice. Together, they organized workshops, advocacy campaigns, and support groups. This partnership expanded the reach and effectiveness of both offices, creating a more inclusive and supportive campus environment.

Innovating Programming

Developing New Programs

Chaplains must continually innovate their programming to meet the evolving needs of students. This includes developing new initiatives that address contemporary issues, such as social justice, environmental sustainability, and digital ethics.

Case Study: Social Justice Advocacy Program

Rabbi Leah developed a social justice advocacy program that provided students with training and resources to engage in social justice work. The program included workshops on activism, community organizing, and ethical leadership. This initiative empowered students to take action on issues they cared about and reinforced the chaplaincy's commitment to social justice.

Fostering Leadership Development

Empowering Student Leaders

Chaplains play a crucial role in fostering leadership development among students. By providing mentorship, leadership training, and opportunities for involvement, chaplains help students develop skills that will benefit them in their personal and professional lives.

Story: Leadership Mentorship Program

Rev. John established a leadership mentorship program for student leaders of faith-based organizations. The program included one-on-one mentorship, leadership workshops, and networking opportunities. This initiative helped students build their leadership skills and fostered a sense of responsibility and service within the campus community.

Adapting to Remote and Hybrid Learning

Supporting Students in Diverse Learning Environments

The shift to remote and hybrid learning models requires chaplains to adapt their support services to meet the needs of students in diverse learning environments. This includes providing virtual resources, maintaining accessibility, and ensuring that all students feel connected and supported.

Case Study: Hybrid Worship Services

Rev. Sarah introduced hybrid worship services that combined in-person and virtual participation. This approach allowed students to join services from anywhere, creating an inclusive and flexible worship experience. The hybrid model ensured that all students, regardless of their physical location, could engage with their faith community.

Evaluating Impact and Effectiveness

Continuously Improving Services

Chaplains must regularly evaluate the impact and effectiveness of their programs and services. By seeking feedback, analyzing outcomes, and making data-informed decisions, chaplains can continuously improve their offerings to better serve the campus community.

Story: Feedback and Improvement Initiative

Dr. Thompson launched a feedback initiative to gather input from students, faculty, and staff about the chaplaincy's programs and services. He used surveys, focus groups, and individual interviews to collect data. The feedback informed several improvements, including new programs and enhanced communication strategies, ensuring that the chaplaincy remained responsive to the community's needs.

The future of campus ministry involves adapting to change and embracing new challenges and opportunities. By responding to increasing diversity, leveraging digital technology, addressing mental health, collaborating with campus partners, innovating programming, fostering leadership development, and supporting students in diverse learning environments, chaplains can continue to provide meaningful and impactful support to the campus community. Through continuous evaluation and improvement, chaplains ensure that their services remain relevant and effective, fostering a supportive and inclusive campus environment.

The role of university chaplains is continually evolving in response to changes in higher education and society. Chaplains must adapt to new challenges and opportunities, such as the increasing diversity of student populations and the rise of digital technology. This chapter explores how chaplains are expanding their roles to include areas like mental health support, social justice advocacy, and environmental stewardship, reflecting the broadening scope of campus ministry.

Expanding Roles

Mental Health Support

Integrating Mental Health and Spiritual Care

As awareness of mental health issues grows, chaplains are increasingly integrating mental health support into their spiritual care. This holistic approach ensures that students receive comprehensive support that addresses both their emotional and spiritual well-being.

Case Study: Mental Health Workshops

Rev. John collaborated with the campus counseling center to offer mental health workshops that combined spiritual practices with mental health strategies. These workshops included mindfulness exercises, stress management techniques, and discussions on the intersection of faith and mental health. The integrated approach provided students with practical tools to manage their mental health while nurturing their spiritual lives.

Providing Crisis Intervention

Supporting Students in Crisis

Chaplains are often on the front lines of providing crisis intervention for students experiencing mental health emergencies. Their training in pastoral care and crisis management equips them to offer immediate support and connect students with professional resources.

Story: Immediate Crisis Support

Imam Rashid received a late-night call from a student in distress. He provided immediate emotional support over the phone and arranged for the student to meet with a counselor the next day. By being accessible and responsive, he played a crucial role in the student's crisis intervention and ongoing support.

Social Justice Advocacy

Championing Social Justice Issues

Chaplains are expanding their roles to include social justice advocacy, and addressing issues such as racial inequality, gender discrimination, and economic injustice. By championing these causes, chaplains help create a more equitable and inclusive campus environment.

Case Study: Racial Justice Initiative

Rabbi Leah led a racial justice initiative on campus that included educational workshops, advocacy campaigns, and partnerships with local organizations. The initiative raised awareness about systemic racism and encouraged the campus community to take action for racial justice. Her leadership in this area highlighted the chaplaincy's commitment to social justice.

Facilitating Difficult Conversations

Encouraging Open Dialogue

Chaplains facilitate difficult conversations about social justice issues, creating safe spaces for dialogue and reflection. These conversations help students understand diverse perspectives and develop a commitment to social change.

Story: Difficult Conversations Forum

Rev. Sarah organized a forum on gender discrimination, where students could share their experiences and discuss solutions. The forum included guided discussions, panel presentations, and small group activities. By fostering open dialogue, she helped students navigate challenging topics and find common ground.

Environmental Stewardship

Promoting Sustainability Initiatives

Chaplains are increasingly involved in promoting environmental stewardship and sustainability initiatives on campus. Their role includes raising awareness about environmental issues, advocating for sustainable practices, and organizing eco-friendly activities.

Case Study: Campus Sustainability Program

Dr. Thompson spearheaded a campus sustainability program that included initiatives such as reducing waste, conserving energy, and promoting sustainable transportation.

He organized events like campus clean-ups, tree-planting ceremonies, and sustainability workshops. His efforts helped create a culture of environmental responsibility on campus.

Integrating Faith and Environmental Ethics

Connecting Spirituality with Environmental Stewardship

Chaplains help students understand the connection between their faith and environmental stewardship. By integrating environmental ethics into their spiritual teachings, chaplains encourage students to view caring for the environment as a moral and spiritual responsibility.

Story: Faith and Environment Seminar

Imam Rashid hosted a seminar on the intersection of faith and environmental ethics. The seminar included discussions on religious teachings about stewardship, practical ways to reduce one's environmental footprint, and the spiritual significance of caring for the Earth. This approach helped students see environmental stewardship as an integral part of their faith practice.

Expanding Pastoral Care

Addressing Diverse Needs

As the needs of the campus community evolve, chaplains are expanding their pastoral care services to address a broader range of issues. This includes offering support for topics such as sexuality, identity, and interfaith relationships.

Case Study: LGBTQ+ Support Group

Rabbi Leah established an LGBTQ+ support group that provided a safe space for students to discuss their experiences and receive support. The group included discussions on identity, faith, and navigating challenges related to being LGBTQ+ on campus. Her inclusive approach ensured that all students felt valued and supported.

Providing Comprehensive Support

Holistic Approach to Pastoral Care

Chaplains adopt a holistic approach to pastoral care, addressing the physical, emotional, and spiritual needs of students. This comprehensive support helps students navigate the complexities of college life and fosters their overall well-being.

Story: Comprehensive Care Initiative

Rev. Sarah launched a comprehensive care initiative that included wellness checks, spiritual direction, and referrals to campus resources. The initiative provided a multi-faceted support system that addressed students' diverse needs, promoting their holistic development and well-being.

Embracing Technology

Leveraging Digital Tools

Chaplains are leveraging digital technology to enhance their outreach and support services. This includes using social media, video conferencing, and online platforms to connect with students and provide virtual care.

Case Study: Virtual Chaplaincy Services

Dr. Thompson introduced virtual chaplaincy services that allowed students to access spiritual support online. The services included virtual counseling sessions, online prayer groups, and digital resources on various spiritual topics. This approach ensured that students could receive support regardless of their location.

Creating Online Communities

Fostering Digital Engagement

Chaplains create online communities that provide a platform for students to connect, share experiences, and support one another. These digital spaces complement in-person interactions and ensure that students can access support in a flexible and convenient manner.

Story: Online Spiritual Community

Imam Rashid established an online spiritual community using social media and a dedicated website. The community featured discussion forums, virtual prayer meetings, and resources on various spiritual topics. This initiative allowed students to engage with their faith and connect with others in a digital environment, enhancing their sense of belonging and support.

The future of campus ministry involves expanding roles to meet the evolving needs of the campus community. By integrating mental health support, championing social justice, promoting environmental stewardship, expanding pastoral care, and embracing technology, chaplains ensure that their services remain relevant and impactful. These expanded roles reflect the broadening scope of campus ministry, enabling chaplains to provide comprehensive and meaningful support to students, faculty, and staff. Through their adaptability and commitment to inclusivity, chaplains continue to foster a supportive and thriving campus environment.

The role of university chaplains is continually evolving in response to changes in higher education and society. Chaplains must adapt to new challenges and opportunities, such as the increasing diversity of student populations and the rise of digital technology. This chapter explores the importance of continuing education for chaplains, emphasizing how ongoing professional development ensures they are well-equipped to serve the campus community effectively.

Continuing Education

Importance of Professional Development

Staying Current with Best Practices

Chaplains engage in continuing education to stay current with best practices in pastoral care, counseling, and interfaith dialogue. This commitment to professional development ensures they can provide the highest level of support and guidance to the campus community.

Case Study: Advanced Pastoral Care Training

Rev. John attended an advanced pastoral care training program that covered the latest techniques in counseling, crisis intervention, and spiritual direction. The training equipped him with new skills and strategies to better support students facing a wide range of challenges. His enhanced capabilities led to more effective and compassionate pastoral care.

Expanding Knowledge in Counseling

Enhancing Counseling Skills

Chaplains often encounter students with diverse and complex needs. Continuing education in counseling helps chaplains enhance their skills and stay updated on new approaches to mental health support, ensuring they can address these needs effectively.

Story: Trauma-Informed Counseling Certification

Imam Rashid pursued a certification in trauma-informed counseling, which provided him with specialized knowledge and tools to support students who have experienced trauma. The certification improved his ability to recognize and respond to trauma-related issues, fostering a safer and more supportive environment for students in need.

Advancing Interfaith Dialogue

Promoting Interfaith Understanding

As campus populations become more diverse, chaplains play a critical role in promoting interfaith dialogue and understanding. Continuing education in this area helps chaplains develop the skills needed to facilitate meaningful conversations and foster mutual respect among different faith traditions.

Case Study: Interfaith Dialogue Workshop

Rabbi Leah participated in an interfaith dialogue workshop that focused on techniques for facilitating discussions between individuals from different religious backgrounds. The workshop included role-playing exercises, case studies, and expert presentations. Her enhanced skills enabled her to lead more effective and inclusive interfaith programs on campus.

Embracing Digital Technology

Leveraging Technology for Ministry

The rise of digital technology has transformed the way chaplains connect with the campus community. Continuing education in digital tools and platforms enables chaplains to enhance their outreach, provide virtual support, and create online communities.

Story: Digital Ministry Course

Rev. Sarah completed a course on digital ministry, which covered topics such as social media engagement, virtual counseling, and online community building. The course equipped her with the skills to effectively use technology in her ministry, allowing her to reach a broader audience and provide flexible support options for students.

Fostering Leadership Development

Training Future Leaders

Chaplains play a crucial role in developing student leaders. Continuing education in leadership training equips chaplains with the knowledge and tools to mentor and empower the next generation of leaders on campus.

Case Study: Leadership Development Program

Dr. Thompson enrolled in a leadership development program that focused on mentoring techniques, leadership theories, and practical applications. The program improved his ability to guide and support student leaders, helping them develop the skills and confidence needed to lead effectively.

Addressing Emerging Issues

Staying Informed on Contemporary Challenges

The landscape of higher education is constantly changing, with new challenges and opportunities emerging regularly. Continuing education helps chaplains stay informed about contemporary issues, ensuring they can respond proactively and effectively.

Story: Workshop on Social Justice Advocacy

Imam Rashid attended a workshop on social justice advocacy, which covered topics such as systemic inequality, activism strategies, and community organizing. The workshop provided him with insights and tools to better support students engaged in social justice work and to advocate for positive change on campus.

Building Professional Networks

Connecting with Peers and Experts

Continuing education provides chaplains with opportunities to connect with peers and experts in their field. These professional networks offer valuable support, resources, and collaboration opportunities.

Case Study: Professional Chaplaincy Conference

Rabbi Leah attended a professional chaplaincy conference where she connected with colleagues from other institutions and learned from leading experts in pastoral care, counseling, and interfaith dialogue. The conference provided her with new ideas and best practices to implement on her campus, as well as a network of supportive peers.

Engaging in Reflective Practice

Reflecting on Professional Growth

Reflective practice is an essential component of continuing education. Chaplains engage in self-reflection to assess their experiences, identify areas for improvement, and set goals for professional growth.

Story: Reflective Journaling Practice

Rev. Sarah incorporated reflective journaling into her professional development routine. She regularly documented her experiences, challenges, and successes in a journal, using these reflections to guide her growth and development as a chaplain. This practice helped her maintain a high standard of care and continuously improve her skills.

Enhancing Cultural Competency

Understanding and Respecting Diversity

Cultural competency is crucial for chaplains serving diverse campus communities. Continuing education in cultural competency helps chaplains understand and respect the varied backgrounds and experiences of students, faculty, and staff.

Case Study: Cultural Competency Certification

Dr. Thompson completed a cultural competency certification program that covered topics such as implicit bias, cultural awareness, and inclusive practices. The certification enhanced his ability to support students from diverse backgrounds and foster an inclusive campus environment.

Ensuring Ethical Practice

Upholding Ethical Standards

Chaplains must adhere to high ethical standards in their work. Continuing education in ethics helps chaplains stay informed about ethical guidelines and best practices, ensuring they maintain integrity and professionalism.

Story: Ethics in Chaplaincy Course

Imam Rashid enrolled in a course on ethics in chaplaincy, which covered topics such as confidentiality, dual relationships, and professional boundaries. The course reinforced his commitment to ethical practice and provided him with strategies to navigate complex ethical dilemmas.

Continuing education is essential for chaplains to stay current with best practices and effectively serve the campus community. By engaging in ongoing professional development, chaplains enhance their skills in pastoral care, counseling, interfaith dialogue, digital ministry, leadership development, cultural competency, and ethics. This commitment to lifelong learning ensures that chaplains remain well-equipped to address the evolving needs of students, faculty, and staff, fostering a supportive and inclusive campus environment.

CHAPTER 12

CONCLUSION

The role of a university chaplain is both challenging and rewarding. Chaplains provide vital spiritual and emotional support to the campus community, fostering an environment of inclusivity, ethical behavior, and mutual respect. As universities continue to evolve, the role of chaplains will remain essential in guiding students, faculty, and staff through their academic and personal journeys. This concluding chapter reflects on the multifaceted contributions of chaplains and underscores their enduring significance in higher education.

The Multifaceted Role of Chaplains

Providing Spiritual Guidance

Nurturing Faith and Spirituality

Chaplains offer spiritual guidance that nurtures the faith and spirituality of students, faculty, and staff. Their presence and support help individuals explore their beliefs, find meaning, and connect with their spiritual traditions.

Case Study: Faith Exploration Group

Rev. John facilitated a faith exploration group where students could discuss their spiritual journeys, ask questions, and seek guidance. This group provided a safe space for spiritual growth and fostered a sense of community among participants. The positive impact on students' spiritual lives highlighted the importance of chaplaincy in nurturing faith.

Offering Emotional Support

Addressing Emotional Well-Being

Chaplains play a critical role in supporting the emotional well-being of the campus community. Through counseling, crisis intervention, and ongoing support, chaplains help individuals navigate personal challenges and find resilience.

Story: Emotional Support During Crisis

Imam Rashid provided crucial emotional support to a student who experienced a family tragedy. By offering a listening ear, empathetic presence, and practical guidance, he helped the student cope with their grief and regain a sense of stability. This support was instrumental in the student's emotional recovery and academic success.

Fostering Inclusivity

Creating a Welcoming Environment

Chaplains are champions of inclusivity, working to create a campus environment where all individuals feel welcomed and respected. Their efforts to celebrate diversity, promote interfaith dialogue, and support marginalized groups contribute to a more inclusive and cohesive community.

Case Study: Inclusive Worship Services

Rabbi Leah organized inclusive worship services that incorporated elements from various faith traditions, allowing students from diverse backgrounds to participate and feel valued. These services fostered a sense of belonging and highlighted the chaplaincy's commitment to inclusivity.

Promoting Ethical Behavior

Upholding Integrity and Respect

Chaplains promote ethical behavior by providing guidance on moral and ethical issues, modeling integrity, and fostering a culture of respect. Their influence encourages the campus community to uphold high ethical standards in their personal and academic lives.

Story: Ethical Leadership Workshop

Rev. Sarah conducted an ethical leadership workshop that equipped student leaders with the tools and principles needed to lead with integrity. The workshop emphasized the importance of ethical decision-making and accountability, reinforcing the chaplaincy's role in promoting ethical behavior.

Supporting Academic Success

Enhancing Academic and Personal Growth

Chaplains support academic success by providing holistic care that addresses the spiritual, emotional, and personal needs of students. Their comprehensive approach helps students thrive academically and develop as well-rounded individuals.

Case Study: Academic Support Group

Dr. Thompson established an academic support group that offered students resources on time management, stress reduction, and study skills, combined with spiritual reflection and support. The group helped students improve their academic performance and overall well-being, demonstrating the chaplaincy's contribution to academic success.

Adapting to Change

Embracing New Challenges

The evolving landscape of higher education requires chaplains to adapt to new challenges and opportunities. By embracing diversity, leveraging technology, and expanding their roles, chaplains continue to meet the changing needs of the campus community.

Story: Digital Ministry Innovation

Imam Rashid embraced digital technology to offer virtual counseling sessions and online spiritual resources. This innovation ensured that students could access support regardless of their location, highlighting the chaplaincy's adaptability and commitment to meeting contemporary needs.

The Enduring Significance of Chaplaincy

Guiding Through Transitions

Supporting Life's Milestones

Chaplains provide guidance and support through significant transitions and milestones in the lives of students, faculty, and staff. Their presence during events such as orientation, graduation, and personal crises underscores their vital role in the university experience.

Case Study: Graduation Blessings

Rabbi Leah offered blessings at graduation ceremonies, celebrating the achievements of graduates and providing spiritual encouragement for their future endeavors.

Her contributions added a meaningful dimension to the ceremonies, marking a significant transition in the lives of graduates.

Building Community

Strengthening Campus Bonds

Chaplains play a pivotal role in building and strengthening the campus community. Through events, programs, and personal interactions, they foster connections, create a sense of belonging, and promote a supportive environment.

Story: Community-Building Retreat

Rev. Sarah organized a community-building retreat that brought together students from various backgrounds for team-building activities, spiritual reflection, and social engagement. The retreat strengthened bonds among participants and reinforced the chaplaincy's role in fostering a cohesive campus community.

Advocating for Justice and Equity

Promoting Social Change

Chaplains advocate for justice and equity, addressing social issues and working towards positive change within the university and beyond. Their advocacy efforts raise awareness, inspire action, and contribute to a more just and equitable society.

Case Study: Social Justice Advocacy Campaign

Dr. Thompson led a social justice advocacy campaign focused on addressing food insecurity among students. The campaign included awareness-raising events, advocacy efforts, and partnerships with local organizations. His leadership highlighted the chaplaincy's commitment to social justice and its impact on the campus community.

The role of a university chaplain is both challenging and rewarding, encompassing a wide range of responsibilities that support the spiritual, emotional, and ethical well-being of the campus community. Chaplains provide vital support, foster inclusivity, promote ethical behavior, and adapt to the evolving needs of higher education. As universities continue to evolve, the role of chaplains will remain essential in guiding students, faculty, and staff through their academic and personal journeys. Their enduring significance lies in their ability to create a supportive, inclusive, and ethical environment where all members of the campus community can thrive.

The role of a university chaplain is both challenging and rewarding. Chaplains provide vital spiritual and emotional support to the campus community, fostering an environment of inclusivity, ethical behavior, and mutual respect. As universities continue to evolve, the role of chaplains will remain essential in guiding students, faculty, and staff through their academic and personal journeys. This concluding chapter reflects on the multifaceted contributions of chaplains and underscores their enduring significance in higher education.

The Multifaceted Role of Chaplains

Providing Spiritual Guidance

Chaplains offer spiritual guidance that nurtures the faith and spirituality of students, faculty, and staff. Their presence and support help individuals explore their beliefs, find meaning, and connect with their spiritual traditions.

Offering Emotional Support

Chaplains play a critical role in supporting the emotional well-being of the campus community. Through counseling, crisis intervention, and ongoing support, chaplains help individuals navigate personal challenges and find resilience.

Fostering Inclusivity

Chaplains are champions of inclusivity, working to create a campus environment where all individuals feel welcomed and respected. Their efforts to celebrate diversity, promote interfaith dialogue, and support marginalized groups contribute to a more inclusive and cohesive community.

Promoting Ethical Behavior

Chaplains promote ethical behavior by providing guidance on moral and ethical issues, modeling integrity, and fostering a culture of respect. Their influence encourages the campus community to uphold high ethical standards in their personal and academic lives.

Supporting Academic Success

Chaplains support academic success by providing holistic care that addresses the spiritual, emotional, and personal needs of students. Their comprehensive approach helps students thrive academically and develop as well-rounded individuals.

Adapting to Change

The evolving landscape of higher education requires chaplains to adapt to new challenges and opportunities. By embracing diversity, leveraging technology, and expanding their roles, chaplains continue to meet the changing needs of the campus community.

The Enduring Significance of Chaplaincy

Guiding Through Transitions

Chaplains provide guidance and support through significant transitions and milestones in the lives of students, faculty, and staff. Their presence during events such as orientation, graduation, and personal crises underscores their vital role in the university experience.

Building Community

Chaplains play a pivotal role in building and strengthening the campus community. Through events, programs, and personal interactions, they foster connections, create a sense of belonging, and promote a supportive environment.

Advocating for Justice and Equity

Chaplains advocate for justice and equity, addressing social issues and working towards positive change within the university and beyond. Their advocacy efforts raise awareness, inspire action, and contribute to a more just and equitable society.

Looking to the Future

Through this book, we have explored the many facets of campus ministry, highlighting the importance of chaplains in creating a holistic educational experience. As we look to the future, it is clear that university chaplains will continue to play a crucial role in shaping the spiritual and ethical landscape of higher education. Their ability to provide comprehensive support, foster inclusivity, and promote ethical behavior ensures that they will remain integral to the well-being and success of the campus community.

The enduring significance of chaplains lies in their unwavering commitment to supporting students, faculty, and staff in their personal and academic journeys. As universities continue to evolve, the role of chaplains will be more important than ever in guiding and nurturing the campus community, ensuring that higher education remains a place of growth, discovery, and transformation.

www.ingramcontent.com/pod-product-compliance
Lightning Source LLC
Chambersburg PA
CBHW061242120726
48001CB00001B/101